Table of Contents
Master Math
Introductory Geometry
Grade 6
Plus practice in decimals, fractions, percents, probability, and logic

Lines

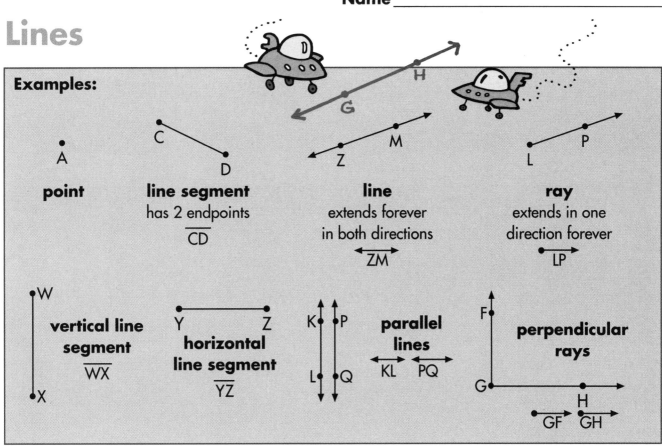

Examples:

point

line segment
has 2 endpoints
$\overline{CD}$

line
extends forever
in both directions
$\overleftrightarrow{ZM}$

ray
extends in one
direction forever
$\overrightarrow{LP}$

vertical line segment
$\overline{WX}$

horizontal line segment
$\overline{YZ}$

parallel lines
$\overleftrightarrow{KL}$ $\overleftrightarrow{PQ}$

perpendicular rays
$\overrightarrow{GF}$ $\overrightarrow{GH}$

Directions: Describe each object using words and symbols.

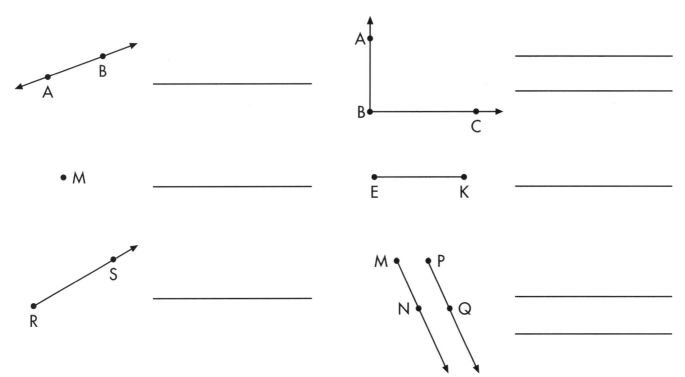

_____

_____
_____

_____

_____

_____

_____
_____

3

What's Your Angle?

Angles can be classified into four groups. They are classified by their angle measures.

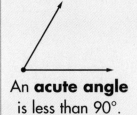

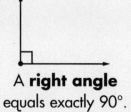

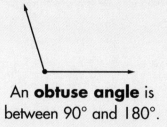

An **acute angle** is less than 90°.

A **right angle** equals exactly 90°.

An **obtuse angle** is between 90° and 180°.

A **straight angle** equals exactly 180°.

Directions: Classify each angle as acute, right, obtuse, or straight.

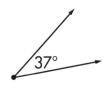
37°

135°

21°

90°

1.

_____   _____   _____   _____

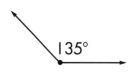
180°

55°

120°

90°

2.

_____   _____   _____   _____

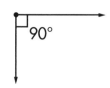

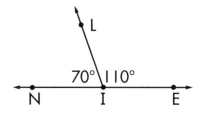

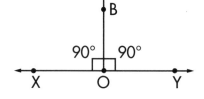

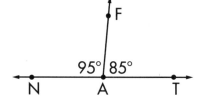

3.

∠LIN _____   ∠BOX _____   ∠FAN _____

∠LIE _____   ∠BOY _____   ∠FAT _____

∠NIE _____   ∠XOY _____   ∠NAT _____

Sail Away With Angles

Directions: Look at each triangle. Use the measurements given to write the kind of triangle on the line (**right**, **acute**, or **obtuse**). Then, find the missing angle. Put the corresponding letter of the angle above its measurement at the bottom of the page to answer the riddle.

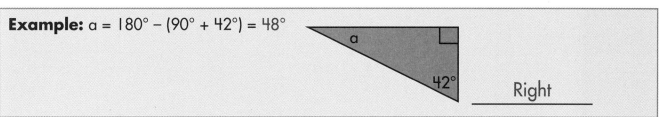

Example: $a = 180° - (90° + 42°) = 48°$

a

42°

_____Right_____

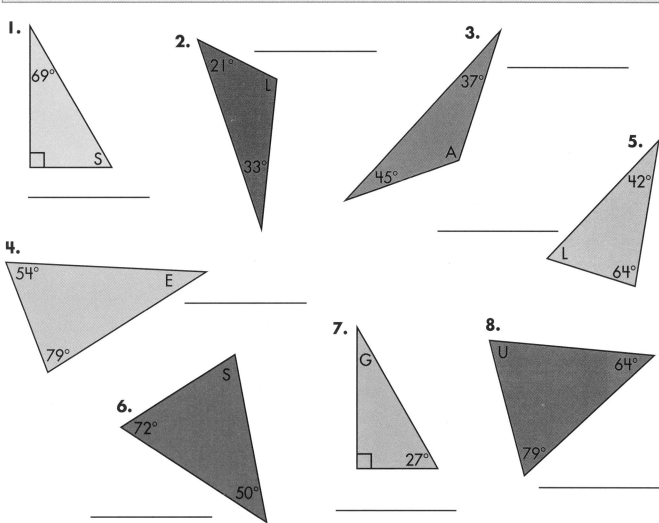

1.

69°

S

_____

2.

_____

21°

L

33°

3.

_____

37°

A

45°

4.

54°

E

79°

_____

5.

42°

L

64°

6.

72°

S

50°

_____

7.

G

27°

_____

8.

U

64°

79°

_____

Which scavenger birds love the water and french fries?

___ ___ ___ ___ ___ ___ ___ ___
21° 47° 98° 63° 37° 74° 126° 58°

Name _____

Star Light, Star Bright

A man was driving a black truck. His lights were not on. The moon was not out. A lady was crossing the street. How did the man see her?

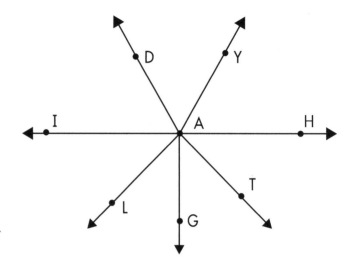

Directions: The answer is hidden in the star picture. Use it to answer the questions.

1. Name an obtuse angle. _____

2. Name a straight angle. _____

3. Find ∠DAG. Name three angles that make up ∠DAG. _____, _____, _____

4. Combine ∠YAH and ∠HAT. What new angle is formed? _____

5. Name three angles that together make up ∠HAL. _____, _____, _____

6. How many angles are hidden within ∠LAY? _____

7. How many right angles can you find? _____

8. Name five angles hidden within ∠IAT.

    _____, _____, _____, _____, _____

9. Name five angles hidden within ∠LAY.

    _____, _____, _____, _____, _____

10. Look at the letters that name all the points. Unscramble them to answer the riddle.

    How did the man see the lady? It was ____ ____ ____ ____ ____ ____ ____ ____!

Mirror, Mirror

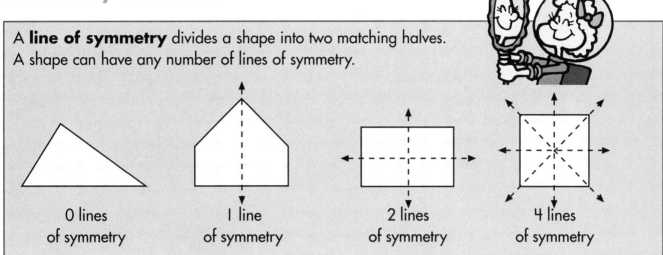

A **line of symmetry** divides a shape into two matching halves.
A shape can have any number of lines of symmetry.

0 lines
of symmetry

1 line
of symmetry

2 lines
of symmetry

4 lines
of symmetry

Directions: Draw all lines of symmetry. If there are none, leave the shape blank.

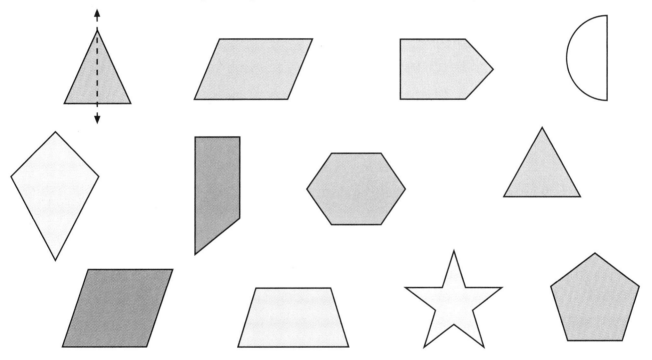

Directions: Draw all lines of symmetry. Symmetry also includes color.

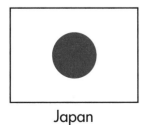

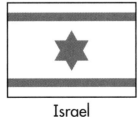

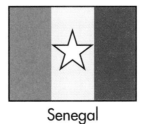

Japan

Israel

Senegal

Guatemala

Master Math: Introductory Geometry

Alike and Different

Shapes are **congruent** if they are exactly the same size and shape.

congruent

Shapes are **similar** if they are about the same relative size.

similar

Directions: Label the shapes in each pair as congruent, similar, or neither.

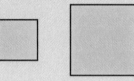

_____

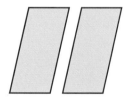

_____

_____

Directions: Use a ruler to draw a congruent and a similar shape for each.

Are all circles similar? _____

Are similar shapes always congruent? _____

Classifying Triangles by Their Sides

Triangles can be classified by the lengths of their sides.

12 m
2 m
13 m

scalene
no equal sides

5 m / 5 m
2 m

isosceles
2 equal sides

Little lines called **hash marks** show sides that are congruent (equal).

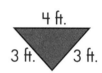
6 m   6 m
6 m

equilateral
3 equal sides

Directions: Write **scalene**, **isosceles**, or **equilateral** to classify each triangle. Draw hash marks (\) to show congruent sides.

1.

10 m   10 m
10 m

_____

12 cm
5 cm
13 cm

_____

4 ft.
3 ft.   3 ft.

_____

2.

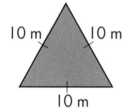
10 yd.
8 yd.
13 yd.

_____

6 m
6 m   6 m

_____

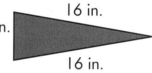
16 in.
4 in.
16 in.

_____

3.

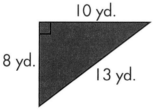
7 cm
7 cm
9 cm

_____

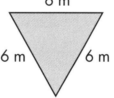
10 m
5 m   8 m

_____

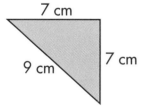
8 ft.   8 ft.
9 ft.

_____

In the space to the right, draw and label an equilateral triangle, an isosceles triangle, and a scalene triangle. Make hash marks to indicate congruent sides.

Classifying Triangles by Their Angles

Triangles can be classified by their angles.

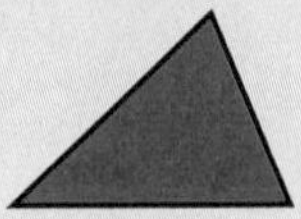

acute triangle
all angles are
acute

equiangular triangle
all angles are
acute and congruent

obtuse triangle
one angle is
an obtuse angle

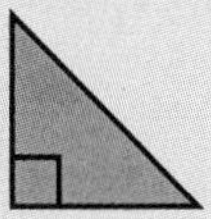

right triangle
one angle is
a right angle

Directions: Write **scalene**, **isosceles**, or **equilateral** to classify each triangle.

1.   80°
45°   75°

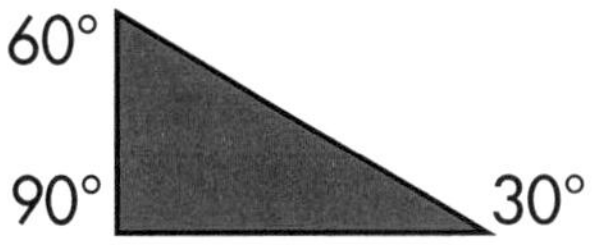

60°
90°   30°

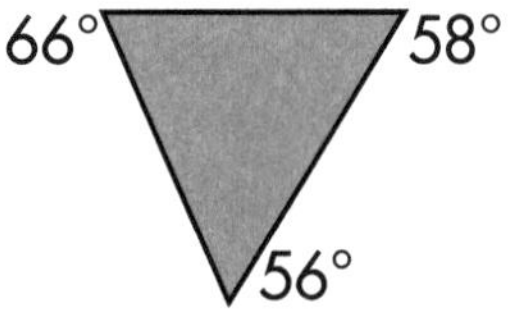

66°   58°
56°

_____   _____   _____

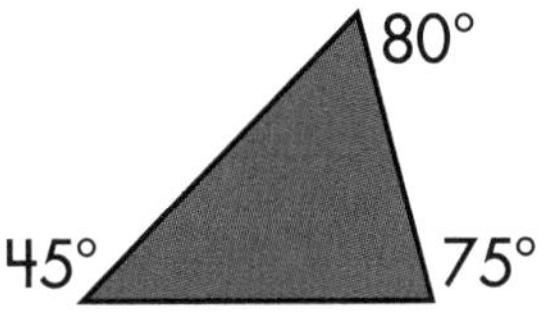

2.   110°
40°   30°

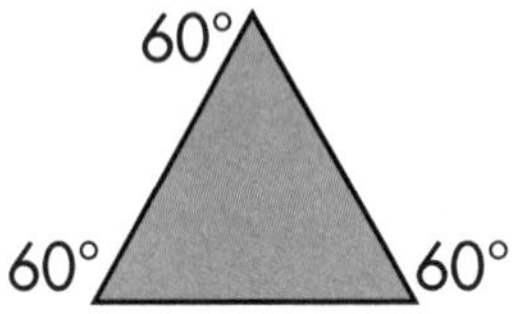

60°
60°   60°

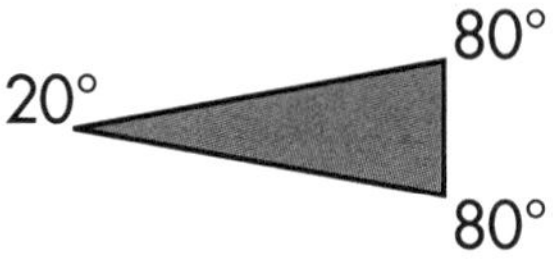

20°   80°
80°

_____   _____   _____

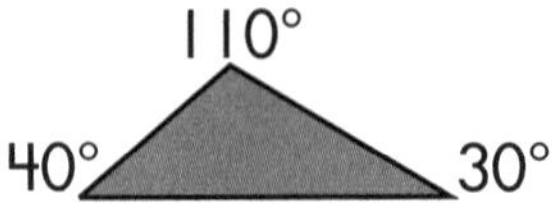

3.   90°
55°   35°

82°
82°   16°

44°   92°
44°

_____   _____   _____

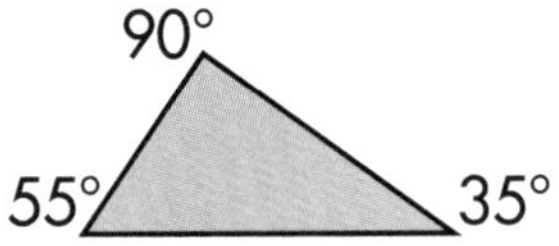

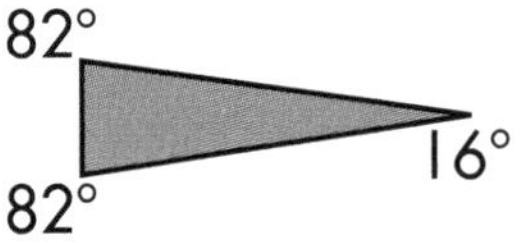

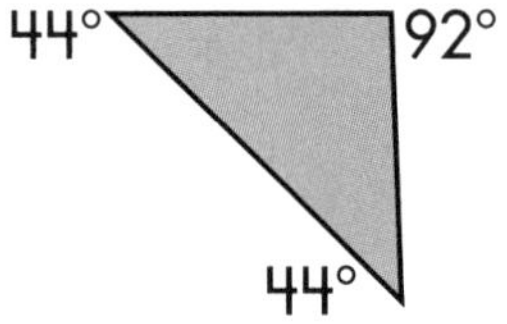

Directions: Draw three different types of triangles. Label each as **acute**, **equiangular**, **right**, or **obtuse**.

_____   _____   _____

Perimeter

Name _____

The **perimeter** is the distance around a shape.

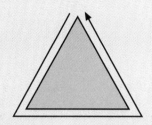 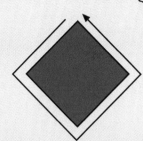 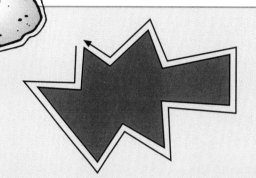

Examples:

Find the perimeter of a polygon by adding the lengths of each side.

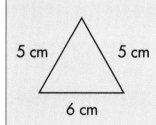

5 cm   5 cm

6 cm

5 + 5 + 6 = 16 cm

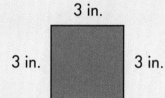

3 in.

3 in.   3 in.

3 in.

3 + 3 + 3 + 3 = 12 in.

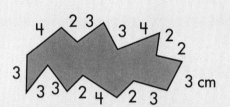

4   2   3   3   4   2

3   2   3 cm

3   3   2   4   2   3

3 + 4 + 2 + 3 + 3 + 4 + 2 + 2 +
3 + 3 + 2 + 4 + 2 + 3 + 3 = 43 cm

Directions: Find the perimeter.

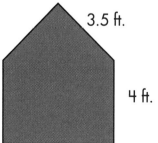

3 cm

7 cm

6 cm

_____

16 in.

12 in.

_____

3.5 ft.

4 ft.

4 ft.

_____

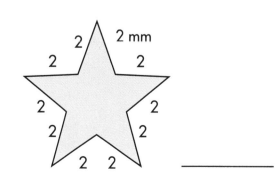

2 mm

2   2   2

2   2

2   2

2   2

_____

 Master Math: Introductory Geometry

Circles

A **circle** is a shape on which all of the points on it are the same distance from a given point. This diagram shows the parts of circle K.

center **K**	the point from which all points on a circle are the same distance
diameter **CD**	a line segment that connects two points on a circle and passes through the center
radius **EK**	a line segment that connects the center with any point on the circle The plural of **radius** is **radii**.
chord **AB**	a line segment that connects two points on a circle but does not pass through the center point

Directions: Read each description below, and write the number of the circle it describes.

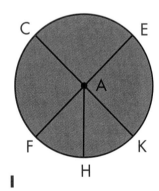

1

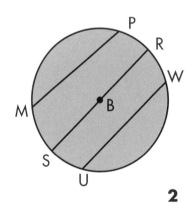

2

Has two chords _____

Has a radius AH _____

Has two diameters _____

Has six radii _____

Has radius CL and CN _____

Has one diameter _____

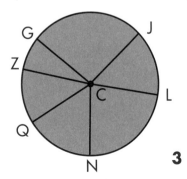

3

The Circle Game

The perimeter of a circle is called the **circumference**. There is a formula for finding the circumference of a circle. The formula uses this special number, **3.14**. We call this number **pi** (π). To find the circumference of a circle, use this formula:

Circumference = π x diameter
Circumference = πd

or

Circumference = π x 2 x radius
Circumference = 2πr

Examples:

C = πd   C = 2πr
C = 3.14 x 4   C = 2 x 3.14 x 2
C = 12.56   C = 12.56

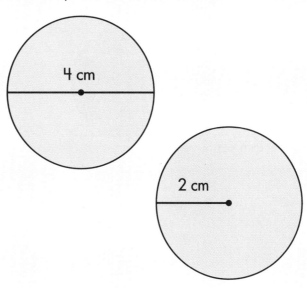

4 cm

2 cm

Directions: Find the circumference for each circle.

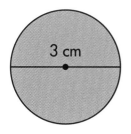

3 cm

25mm

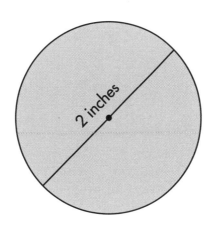

2 inches

_____

_____

_____

Master Math: Introductory Geometry

Waterlogged

What is the largest body of water on Earth?

Directions: To find out, calculate the circumference of each circle. Use your answers to break the code at the bottom of the page. (Use 3.14 for π.)

F.
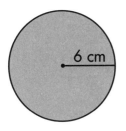
6 cm

_____

P.
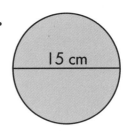
2.5 cm

_____

I.
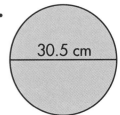
15 cm

_____

O.
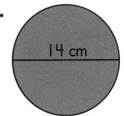
30.5 cm

_____

C.
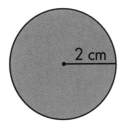
2 cm

_____

E.
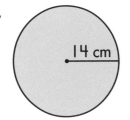
14 cm

_____

T.
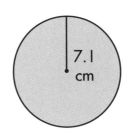
7.1 cm

_____

A.
14 cm

_____

N.
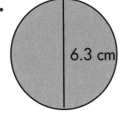
6.3 cm

_____

H.
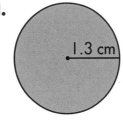
1.3 cm

_____

44.588 cm	8.164 cm	43.96 cm

7.85 cm	43.96 cm	12.56 cm	47.1 cm	37.68 cm	47.1 cm	12.56 cm

95.77 cm	12.56 cm	87.92 cm	43.96 cm	19.782 cm

Exploring Circumference and Diameter

Study the definitions in the term box and look closely at the circle to understand and answer the questions below.

Terms

Circumference: the distance around a circle

Diameter: a segment connecting two points on a circle and going through the center of the circle

Radius: a line segment connecting the center of a circle to any point on the circle

Central Angle: an angle whose vertex is at the center of a circle

Center: a point such that every point on the circle is the same distance from it

Chord: any line segment that connects two points on a circle

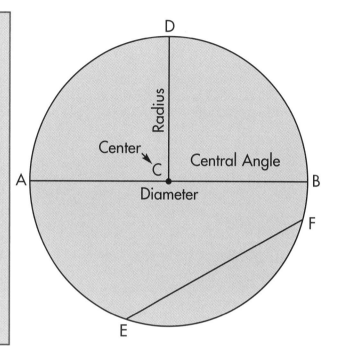

Directions: List the line segments for the following. Remember to draw a line over the two letters to represent a segment. For example: $\overline{NO}$

1. Radius:_____

2. Diameter:_____

3. Chord: _____

4. What is the measurement of the central

   angle? _____

5. If the radius is 3.5 feet, what is the

   diameter? _____

6. If the diameter is 4 feet and 12 inches, what is the radius?

   _____

7. If the radius is 9 yards, how many inches is the diameter?

   _____

8. If the diameter is 4 feet and 18 inches, how long is the radius?

   _____

Formula One

To find the **area** of a square or rectangle, multiply the length by the width.

Example:

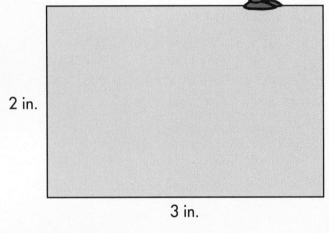

Area = 2 in. x 3 in.
= 6 square in.
= 6 in.^{2}

Area of a square = side x side = s x s = s^2

Area of a rectangle = length x width = l x w = lw

Directions: Find the area of each shape.

10 ft.

10 cm   3 cm

3 in.   1 in.

_____   _____   _____

14 mm   7 mm

1.5 m

16 cm   12 cm   20 cm

_____   _____   _____

Area of Rectangles and Squares

To find the **area** (A) of any rectangle, multiply its length times its width. Remember that a square is a rectangle.

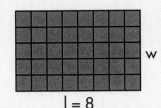

w = 5
l = 8

A = length • width
A = 8 • 5
A = 40 u²

Directions: Find the area of each square or rectangle. Write your answers in square units.

1.

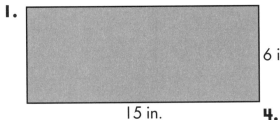

6 in.

15 in.

A = ___90 in.²___

2.

12.2 yd.

8 yd.

A = _____

4.

6.2 ft.

8.7 ft.

A = _____

3.

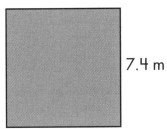

7.4 m

A = _____

5.

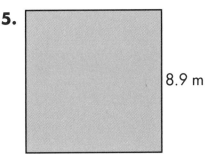

8.9 m

A = _____

6.

3.8 dm

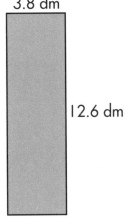

12.6 dm

A = _____

7.

12 cm

17 cm

A = _____

8.

10.6 mm

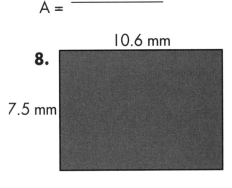

7.5 mm

A = _____

An A-peel-ing Riddle

What shapes are made from banana peels?

Directions: To find out, find the area of each shape. Use the formulas to help you. Then, use your answers to break the code at the bottom of the page.

S.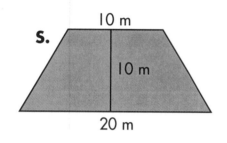
10 m
10 m
20 m

_____

Area of trapezoid
$\frac{1}{2} h(b_1 + b_2)$

Area of triangle
$\frac{1}{2} bh$

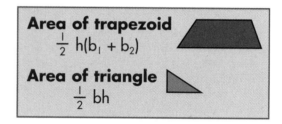

E.
22 m
12 m

R.
10.5 m
42 m

_____

P.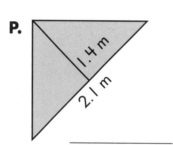
1.4 m
2.1 m

_____

L.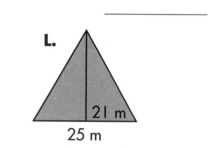
21 m
25 m

_____

S.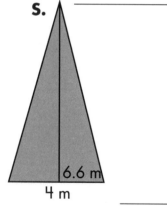
6.6 m
4 m

P.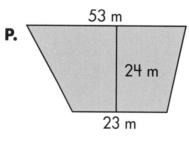
53 m
24 m
23 m

_____

I.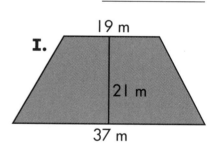
19 m
21 m
37 m

_____

_____ _____ _____ _____ _____ _____ _____ _____
13.2 m²   262.5 m²   588 m²   1.47 m²   912 m²   132 m²   220.5 m²   150 m²

Master Math: Introductory Geometry

18

©2006 School Specialty Publishing

Area

Triangle:	area = $\frac{1}{2}$ base x height
Rectangle/Square:	area = base x height
Parallelogram:	area = base x height
Trapezoid:	area = $\frac{1}{2}$ height (base + base)

Directions: Find the area of the polygonal regions below. Express in square units.

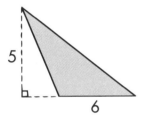

1. _____

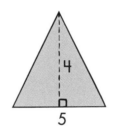

2. _____

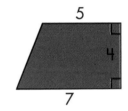

3. _____

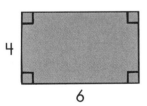

4. _____

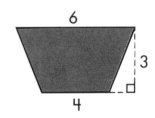

5. _____

6. _____

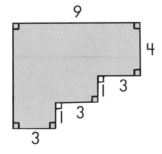

7. _____

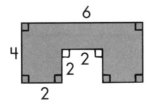

8. _____

Compound Figures

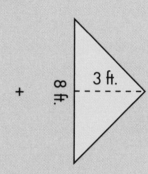

Shapes created by combining two or more polygons are called **compound figures**. To find the area of a compound figure, divide it into shapes with known areas such as triangles, circles, and squares. Then, find the area of each shape and add or subtract.

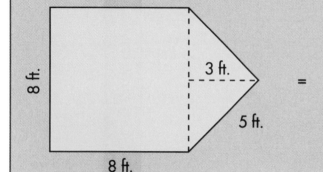

A = 64 ft.² + 12 ft.²
= 76 ft.²

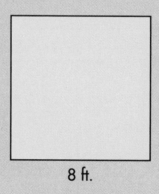

A = 8 ft. x 8 ft.
= 64 ft.²

A = ½ (8 x 3)
= 12 ft.²

Directions: Find the area (the number of square feet) of the shaded area.

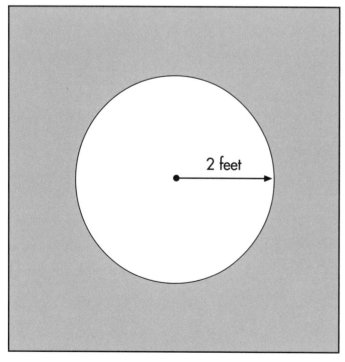

8 feet

Area of the square = _____

Area of the circle = _____

Shaded area = _____

Area of Parallelograms

To find the area of a parallelogram, multiply its base times its height.

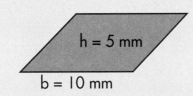

$A = b \cdot h$
$A = 10 \text{ mm} \cdot 5 \text{ mm}$
$A = 50 \text{ mm}^2$

Directions: Find the area of each parallelogram. Write your answers in square units.

1.

h = 3 mm
b = 12 mm

A = _____

2.

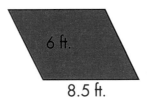

6 ft.

8.5 ft.

A = _____

3.

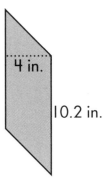

4 in.

10.2 in.

A = _____

4.

1.8 cm
12.2 cm

A = _____

5.

5 yd.
6.3 yd.

A = _____

6.

4.8 m

16 m

A = _____

7.

23.4 ft.
9.4 ft.

A = _____

8.

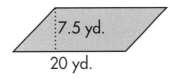

7.5 yd.
20 yd.

A = _____

Area of Trapezoids

To find the area of a trapezoid, use the formula $\frac{1}{2}$ (base$_1$ + base$_2$) • height.

$A = \frac{1}{2} (b_1 + b_2) • h$

$A = \frac{1}{2} (10 + 12) • 6$

$A = \frac{1}{2} (22 • 6)$

$A = 66$ ft.^{2}

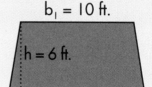

$b_1 = 10$ ft.

$h = 6$ ft.

$b_2 = 12$ ft.

Directions: Write an equation using the formula $\frac{1}{2}$ (b$_1$ + b$_2$) • h. Use it to find the area of each trapezoid. Work on scratch paper. Write your answers in square units.

1.

7 in.

4 in.

10 in.

A = _____

2.

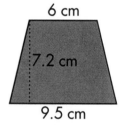

2.5 yd.

5 yd.   7 yd.

A = _____

3.

6 cm

7.2 cm

9.5 cm

A = _____

4.

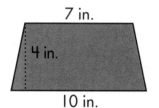

8 mm   5 mm   3.5 mm

A = _____

5.

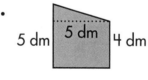

5 dm   5 dm   4 dm

A = _____

6.

16 cm

11 cm

13 cm

A = _____

7.

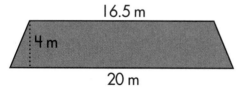

16.5 m

4 m

20 m

A = _____

8.

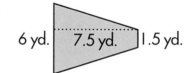

6 yd.   7.5 yd.   1.5 yd.

A = _____

Mad Measurements

What can be measured but has no length, width, or thickness?

Directions: To find out, calculate the missing measurements below. Write the corresponding letters with the answers at the bottom of the page. All measurements are cm.

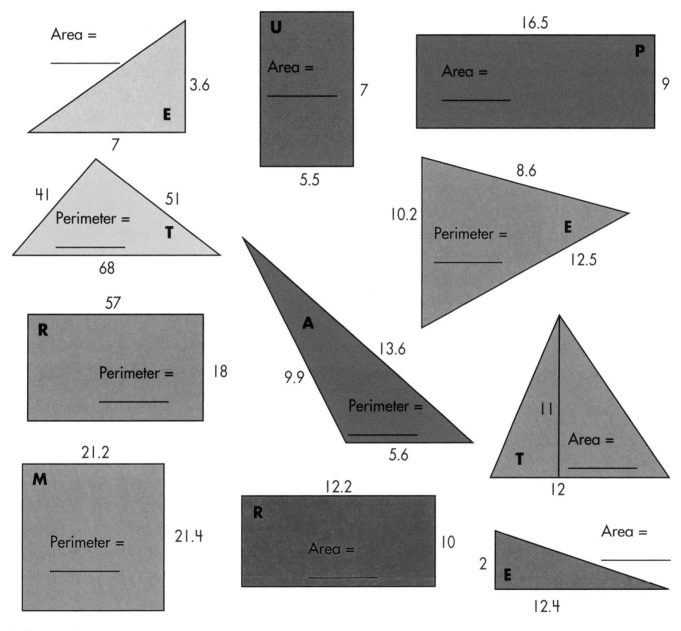

What is it?

____ ____ ____ ____ ____ ____ ____ ____ ____ ____ ____!
66   12.6   85.2   148.5   12.4   150   29.1   160   38.5   122   31.3

To the Edge

Name _____

Polyhedra can be described by the number of faces, edges, and vertices (a vertex is where three edges meet) they have.

A cube has 6 faces, 8 vertices, and 12 edges.

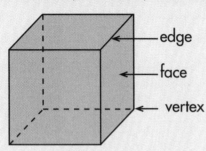

- ← edge
- ← face
- ← vertex

Directions: Write the number of faces, edges, and vertices for each shape.

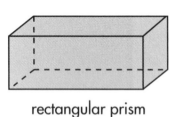

rectangular prism

faces _____

edges _____

vertices _____

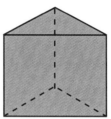

triangular prism

faces _____

edges _____

vertices _____

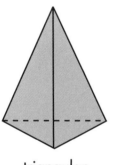

triangular
pyramid

faces _____

edges _____

vertices _____

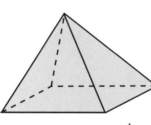

square pyramid

faces _____

edges _____

vertices _____

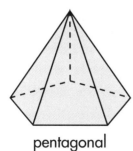

pentagonal
pyramid

faces _____

edges _____

vertices _____

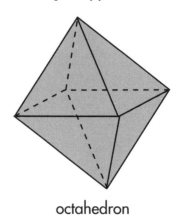

octahedron

faces _____

edges _____

vertices _____

Name _____

Pump Up the Volume!

The **volume** of a 3-D shape is the amount of space it occupies. Volume is measured in cubic units, such as cubic centimeters (cm³) or cubic inches (in.³).

Imagine a box filled with unit cubes. The number of cubes is the volume of the box.

The box has a volume of 16 cubic units.

Directions: Find the volume of each shape in cubic units.

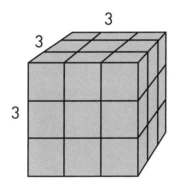

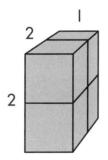

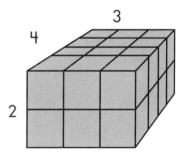

_____   _____   _____

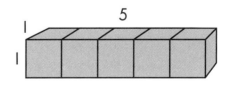

_____   _____

           Master Math: Introductory Geometry

How Much Does It Hold?

Directions: Find the volume of each figure. Use the formula
Volume = length x width x height. You may use a calculator if you have one.

Remember to write your answer in cubic units.

5 cm
3 cm
4 cm
V = 4 x 3 x 5 = 60 cm³

1.

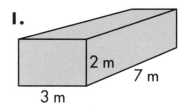

2 m
7 m
3 m

V = _____

2.

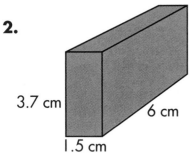

3.7 cm
6 cm
1.5 cm

V = _____

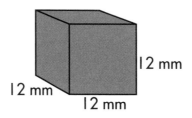

10 in.
8 in.
15 in.

V = _____

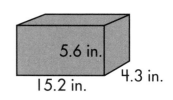

4 yd.
12 yd.
6.1 yd.

V = _____

3.

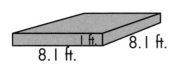

1 ft.
8.1 ft.
8.1 ft.

V = _____

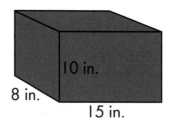

12 mm
12 mm
12 mm

V = _____

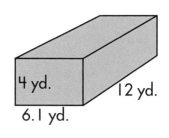

5.6 in.
4.3 in.
15.2 in.

V = _____

4.

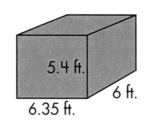

12.4 m
5 m
6.8 m

V = _____

5.4 ft.
6 ft.
6.35 ft.

V = _____

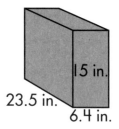

15 in.
23.5 in.
6.4 in.

V = _____

Volume Variation

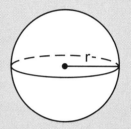

To find the volume of a **cylinder**, a **pyramid**, and a **sphere**, follow these directions:

volume of a cylinder	volume of a pyramid	volume of a sphere

V = area of base x height
   = $\pi r^2 h$

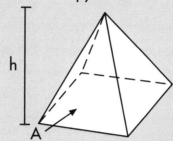

V = area of base x height x $\frac{1}{3}$
   = $\frac{1}{3} Ah$

$V = \frac{4}{3} \pi r^3$

Directions: Find the volume of each shape.

3 in.
5 in.

$\underline{\quad v = (\pi) \times 3 \times 3 \times 5 \quad}$

$\underline{\quad v = 45\pi = 141.3 \text{ in.}^3 \quad}$

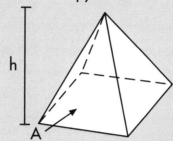
3 ft.

_____

_____

6 cm
4 cm

_____

_____

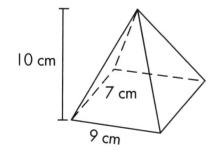
10 cm
7 cm
9 cm

_____

_____

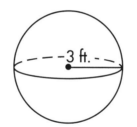
4 m
1 m

_____

_____

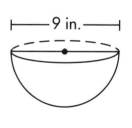
9 in.

_____

_____

     Master Math: Introductory Geometry

Graphing in Four Quadrants

To graph an ordered pair, start at the origin, (0, 0). Move **x** units right or left. Then, move **y** units up or down.

The ★ is at point (−1,−4). Since both numbers are negative (−), it is in Quadrant III.

To plot this point, you would
    Start at the origin.
    Move 1 unit to the left.
    Move 4 units down.

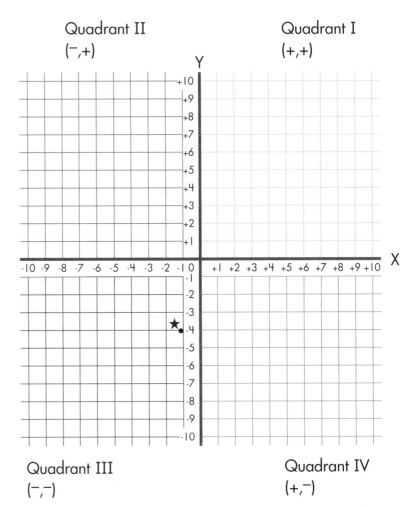

Quadrant II
(−,+)

Quadrant I
(+,+)

Quadrant III
(−,−)

Quadrant IV
(+,−)

Directions: Draw and label each point at the given location.

1. (3,4)	**2.** (−2,5)	**3.** (4,7)	**4.** (5,−6)
5. (−6,−8)	**6.** (−5,7)	**7.** (−4,−5)	**8.** (10,6)
9. (7,9)	**10.** (−2,−8)	**11.** (−10,−3)	**12.** (5,5)
13. (9,6)	**14.** (−4,−9)	**15.** (−9,2)	**16.** (8,−4)

Directions: Draw and label a point in each quadrant. Write the location of each point.

Quadrant I   Quadrant II   Quadrant III   Quadrant IV

Q _____   R _____   S _____   T _____

Decimal Drawings

Decimals represent numbers that include a part of a whole. With decimals, the part that is less than 1 is always separated into 10, or a power of 10, parts.

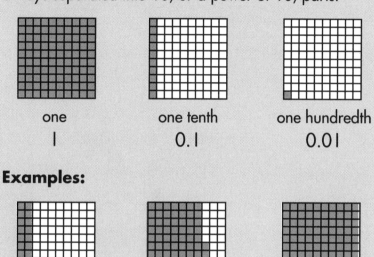

one	one tenth	one hundredth
1	0.1	0.01

Examples:

0.2   0.75   1.00

Directions: Write the decimal number that shows the part that is shaded.

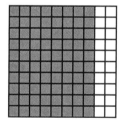   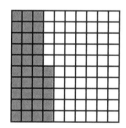   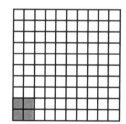   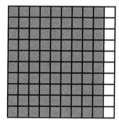

_____   _____   _____   _____

Directions: Shade the diagrams to show the decimal number.

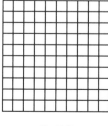   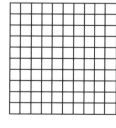   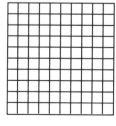

0.50   0.02   0.93   0.15

That's the Point

When writing a decimal, place the decimal point between the ones column and the tenths column. Here are some place values to the right and left of the decimal point.

| hundreds | tens | ones | tenths | hundredths | thousandths |

Steps:

1. Read the whole number.

2. Say the word "and" or "point."

3. Read the number after the decimal point.

4. Say the decimal place of the last digit to the right.

Examples:

45.91 is read "forty-five and ninety-one hundredths"
222.1 is read "two hundred twenty-two point one"
10.004 is read "ten and four thousandths"

Directions: Fill in the numbers or write the names to complete the place-value chart.

HUNDREDS TENS ONES TENTHS HUNDREDTHS THOUSANDTHS

1 ☐ . 8   eleven and eight tenths

3 . ☐ ☐ 1   three and one hundred forty-one thousandths

☐ . ☐ ☐   two and fifteen hundredths

4 0 5 . ☐ ☐ ☐   four hundred five and fifty-six thousandths

☐ . ☐ ☐   forty-eight hundredths

5 6 . 1 1 1   _____

☐ ☐ . ☐ ☐   ninety-eight and three hundredths

April Showers

Comparing and ordering decimals is similar to working with whole numbers.

Example:

Put 6.529, 6.531, and 6.526 in order from greatest to least.

Steps:

1. Align the numbers along the decimal point.
   6.529
   6.531
   6.526

2. Work from left to right. In this problem, start by comparing the ones place.

3. If all the digits are the same, move to the next place.

4. In the hundredths place, 3 > 2 so 6.531 is the greatest number.

5. In the thousandths place, 9 > 6 so 6.529 is greater than 6.526.

6. 531, 6.529, and 6.526 are in order from greatest to least.

Directions: Select 5 meteors with decimal numbers that fall between the two numbers on the rockets. Order them from least to greatest, and write them on the planet.

Compare the Decimals

Directions: Write **>**, **<**, or **=** in each ◯.

1. 6.5 ◯ 6.4   0.95 ◯ 0.96   7.40 ◯ 7.4

2. 0.86 ◯ 0.859   9.02 ◯ 9.20   8.51 ◯ 8.5

3. 12.6 ◯ 1.26   6.18 ◯ 6.20   0.03 ◯ 0.3

4. 1.863 ◯ 1.862   4.32 ◯ 4.23   5.2 ◯ 5.1999

5. 3.046 ◯ 3.406   7.419 ◯ 6.42   45.3 ◯ 45.28

6. 45.3 ◯ 45.28   14.602 ◯ 14.62   1.1406 ◯ 1.146

7. 82.9 ◯ 83.0   11.060 ◯ 11.06   3.064 ◯ 3.064

8. 0.523 ◯ 0.530   12.0 ◯ 11.91   1.351 ◯ 13.51

Directions: Write the decimals from the least to the greatest on the ladders. Start at the bottom.

8.357, 8.35, 8.361, 8.36   12.310, 12.301, 12.013, 12.130

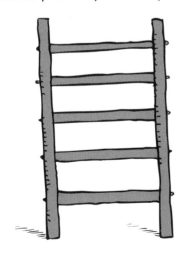

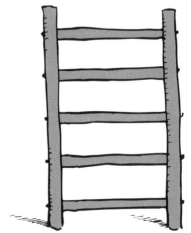

In the Sky

Name _____

Directions: Complete each number to make the expression true.

1. 0.30____9 < 0.3019   0.____45 >0.29   34.3____ < 35.37

2. 16.788 < 16.7____8   8.42____ > 8.427   ____.067 < 1.0671

3. 3.416 > ____.416   28.____47 < 28.147   0.03243 < 0.03____2

4. 5.345 > 5.____45   0.06____83 < 0.06184   178.____71 > 178.789

5. 3.99____ < 3.999   2.527 > 2.____48   17.098 > 1____.908

6. 2.0____3 >1.999   17.6 > 1.____06   2____7.095 < 217.099

Directions: Write the decimals in order from least to greatest.

7. 16.39; 16.8; 16.7; 16.79

8. 72.59; 56.56; 73.1; 56.6; 72.48

9. 0.06; 0.6; 6.060; 0.006

10. 109.041; 104.091; 401.001

11. 5.5508; 5.5880; 5.58; 5.56

May Flowers

Rounding decimals is the same as rounding whole numbers.

Example:

Round 4.386 to the nearest tenth.

Steps:

1. Underline the place to round to and look at the   4.<u>3</u>86
    digit one place to the right.

2. If this digit is less than 5, the digit you are rounding to stays the same.
    If the digit you are rounding to is greater than or equal to 5, add 1 to the place value.

    4.386 is 4.4 rounded to the nearest tenth.

Directions: Round the numbers on each flower to the nearest ones, tenths, and hundredths. Write the rounded numbers on the petals.

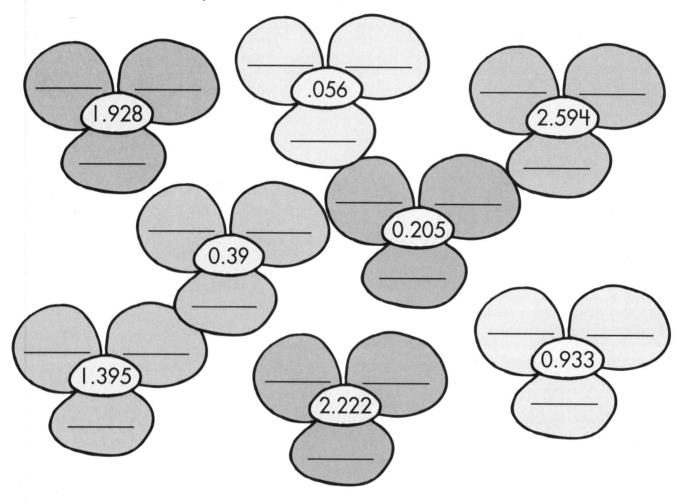

Order, Please!

Directions: Frank worked for his sister at the school snack shop. In one hour, he took orders for 20 items. He had to keep track of prices in his head, so he decided to round the prices. Help Frank round each price. Write the number on the price tag.

1. Round to the nearest dollar.

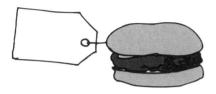

$1.44
hamburger

$1.63
ham sandwich

$2.37
jumbo french fries

2. Round to the nearest tenth.

$2.46
apple pie

$0.34
peach

$1.19
strawberries

3. Round to the nearest whole number.

$6.35
special meal deal

$12.59
value meal

$5.99
hot dog meal

4. Round to the nearest whole number.

$1.29
jumbo popcorn

$2.54
giant cookie

$0.62
brownie

Adding Decimals

Adding decimals is a lot like adding whole numbers.
Be sure to align the decimal points.

CORRECT

$$5.349$$
$$+ 34.322$$
$$\overline{39.671}$$

INCORRECT

$$5.349$$
$$+ 34.322$$
$$\overline{87.812}$$

If the numbers being added do not have the same
number of decimal places, write an equivalent decimal.
Equivalent decimals are two decimals with the same value.

Examples: $0.29 = 0.290$ $1.4 = 1.400$ $3 = 3.000$

Adding zeros to the right of the last decimal digit does not change the value of the number.

Example: $13.83 + 1.264 \longrightarrow$ 13.830
$$+ \ 1.264$$
$$\overline{15.094}$$

Directions: If all the decimals are equivalent, write a ✔ in the box. If not, write an **X**.

4.2	4.20	4.200	☐	3.05	3.5	3.005	☐
0.080	0.08	0.0800	☐	9.000	9	9.0	☐
0.77	0.7	0.777	☐	1.6	1.06	1.60	☐

Directions: Write an equivalent decimal for each number.

1.9 _____   0.040 _____   8 _____   0.3 _____

7.82 _____   4.02 _____   0.90 _____   5 _____

Subtracting Decimals

Steps:

1. Align the decimal points.

2. Write an equivalent number if necessary.

3. Subtract as with whole numbers.

Examples:

$$15.865 - 3.272 \rightarrow \begin{array}{r} 15.865 \\ -\ 3.272 \\ \hline 12.593 \end{array}$$

$$3.44 - 0.538 \rightarrow \begin{array}{r} 3.440 \\ -\ 0.538 \\ \hline 2.902 \end{array}$$

$$2 - 1.894 \rightarrow \begin{array}{r} 2.000 \\ -\ 1.894 \\ \hline 0.106 \end{array}$$

Directions: Subtract the lesser number from the greater one. Show your work in the space below.

1.11	1.111	_____	1.321	4.4	_____
0.41	0.001	_____	8.39	7	_____
12.304	12.403	_____	107.65	67.293	_____
4	2.078	_____	3.7	106.35	_____
0.89	1.6	_____	0.034	0.034	_____

Multiplying Decimals

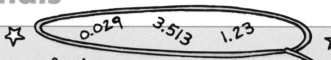

Steps:

1. Ignore the decimal point, and multiply as with whole numbers.

2. Count the number of decimal places in both factors.

3. Place the decimal point that many places from the right in the product.

Examples:

$$0.46 \longrightarrow \text{2 decimal places}$$
$$\underline{\times \quad 0.9} \longrightarrow \text{1 decimal place}$$
$$0.414 \longrightarrow \text{3 decimal places}$$

Directions: Multiply. Show your work in the space below.

1.2 x 0.4 _____   0.5 x 0.1 _____   1.1 x 0.73 _____

0.6 x 0.3 _____   1.5 x 0.4 _____   14.5 x 0.23 _____

2.4 x 1.8 _____   0.82 x 0.2 _____   0.09 x 0.4 _____

Dividing Decimals

Steps:

1. Move the decimal point in the divisor to the right enough places to make it a whole number.

2. Move the decimal point in the dividend the same number of places to the right. Add zeros if necessary.

3. Divide as with whole numbers.

4. Place the decimal point in the quotient directly above it in the dividend.

Examples:

$13.608 ÷ 2.4$　　　　$0.169 ÷ 0.65$　　　　$4 ÷ 0.002$　　　　$1 ÷ 8$

$$\begin{array}{r} 5.67 \\ 2.4\overline{\smash{)}13.6\,08} \end{array}$$　　$$\begin{array}{r} 0.26 \\ 0.65\overline{\smash{)}0.16\,90} \end{array}$$　　$$\begin{array}{r} 2\,000 \\ 0.002\overline{\smash{)}4.000.} \end{array}$$　　$$\begin{array}{r} 0.125 \\ 8\overline{\smash{)}1.000} \end{array}$$

Directions: Divide each dividend on the left by both divisors. Write the quotients and circle the larger answer.

$1.2 ÷$　　$0.3 \ = \ $ _____

　　　　$0.4 \ = \ $ _____

$0.96 ÷$　$0.4 \ = \ $ _____

　　　　$0.06 = \ $ _____

$0.243 ÷$　$0.9 \ = \ $ _____

　　　　$3 \ = \ $ _____

$5 ÷$　　$2.5 \ = \ $ _____

　　　　$4 \ = \ $ _____

$0.04 ÷$　$0.2 \ = \ $ _____

　　　　$0.04 = \ $ _____

$2.88 ÷$　$0.16 = \ $ _____

　　　　$0.18 = \ $ _____

$0.016 ÷$　$0.8 \ = \ $ _____

　　　　$0.08 = \ $ _____

$0.2 ÷$　$0.8 \ = \ $ _____

　　　　$1 \ = \ $ _____

Fractions and Decimals

Fractions and decimals are two related ways of writing numbers. The amount shaded in these pictures can be shown as a decimal or a fraction.

$\frac{7}{10}$ or 0.7

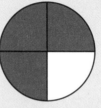

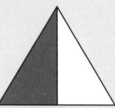

$\frac{7}{10}$ or 0.7 $\frac{24}{100}$ or 0.24 $\frac{3}{4}$ or 0.75 $\frac{1}{2}$ or 0.5

Any fraction can be rewritten as a decimal. To rewrite a fraction as a decimal, divide the denominator into the numerator.

Examples:

$$\frac{3}{4} \rightarrow 4\overline{)3.00}^{\,0.75} = 0.75 \qquad \frac{9}{20} \rightarrow 20\overline{)9.00}^{\,0.45} = 0.45$$

$$\frac{8}{100} \rightarrow 100\overline{)8.00}^{\,0.08} = 0.08 \qquad \frac{62}{250} \rightarrow 250\overline{)62.000}^{\,0.248} = 0.248$$

To change a mixed number to a decimal, change the fraction part to a decimal and add it to the whole number.

$$4\frac{3}{5} = 4 + \frac{3}{5} = 4 + (3 \div 5) = 4 + 0.6 = 4.6$$

$$1\frac{7}{8} = 1 + \frac{7}{8} = 1 + (7 \div 8) = 1 + 0.875 = 1.875$$

Directions: Rewrite each fraction as a decimal.

$\frac{1}{2}$

$\frac{4}{5}$

$\frac{3}{10}$

$\frac{3}{8}$

The Big Island

To write a decimal as a fraction, write the decimal as a fraction with a denominator of 10, 100, 1,000, or another multiple of ten.

Examples:

0.4 = four tenths = $\frac{4}{10}$

1.29 = one and twenty-nine hundredths = $1\frac{29}{100}$ or $\frac{129}{100}$

0.005 = five thousandths = $\frac{5}{1000}$

4.804 = four and eight hundred four thousandths = $4\frac{804}{1000}$ or $\frac{4804}{1000}$

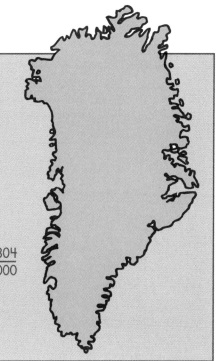

Directions: What is the largest island in the world? Write the letter for each fraction above its matching decimal to decode the answer.

A = $\frac{7}{10}$ **B** = $2\frac{5}{10}$ **C** = 196   **U** = $\frac{7}{100}$ **Y** = $\frac{9}{1000}$

F = $\frac{9}{10}$ **P** = $1\frac{4}{100}$ **H** = $\frac{25}{100}$ **I** = $1\frac{6}{10}$ **K** = $\frac{4}{5}$

L = $1\frac{96}{100}$ **M** = $\frac{16}{10}$ **N** = $\frac{25}{1000}$ **G** = $1\frac{4}{1000}$ **R** = $\frac{16}{100}$

S = 45   **T** = $\frac{196}{1000}$ **D** = $\frac{9}{100}$ **W** = $\frac{4}{10}$ **E** = $\frac{45}{10}$

$\overline{}$ $\overline{}$ $\overline{}$ $\overline{}$ $\overline{}$ $\overline{}$ $\overline{}$ $\overline{}$ $\overline{}$
1.004   0.16   4.5   4.5   0.025   1.96   0.7   0.025   0.09

Decimals

Directions: Change each decimal to a fraction or mixed numeral.

	a.	b.	c.
1.	.9 = _____	.01 = _____	1.005 = _____
2.	.07 = _____	9.003 = _____	.06 = _____
3.	8.62 = _____	.85 = _____	.002 = _____
4.	.03 = _____	7.001 = _____	4.7 = _____
5.	.33 = _____	.006 = _____	.02 = _____
6.	5.09 = _____	.5 = _____	6.004 = _____
7.	.04 = _____	.08 = _____	.467 = _____
8.	2.2 = _____	.15 = _____	3.05 = _____

Giving 100%

Examples:

The word **percent** means "for each hundred." A test score of 95% means that 95 out of 100 answers are correct.

There are 100 squares in this grid. Each square represents one hundredth. Since 63 squares are shaded, 63% is shaded.

Directions: Write the percent of squares shaded.   Shade each grid to show the percent.

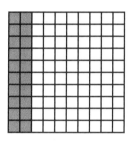 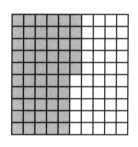 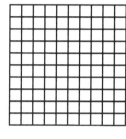 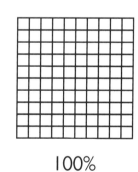

_____   _____   45%   10%

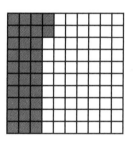 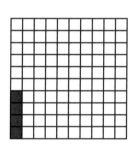 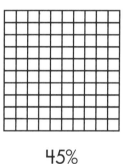 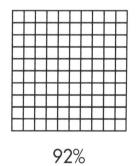

_____   _____   92%   100%

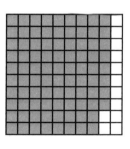 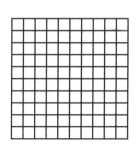 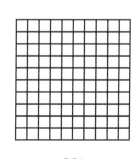 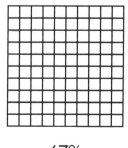

_____   _____   8%   67%

Decimals, Fractions, and Percents

Decimals, fractions, and percents are different ways of representing the same number.

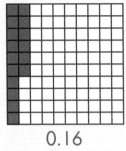
0.16
(sixteen hundredths)

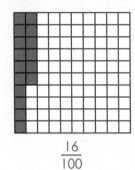
$\frac{16}{100}$
(or $\frac{4}{25}$ in simplest form)

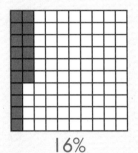
16%

Directions: Write the amount shaded as a decimal, a fraction in the simplest form, and a percent.

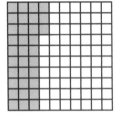
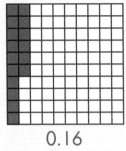
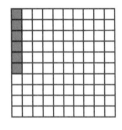
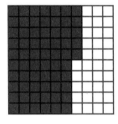

___ ___ ___   ___ ___ ___   ___ ___ ___   ___ ___ ___

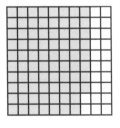
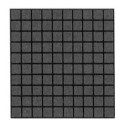
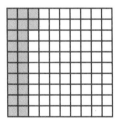
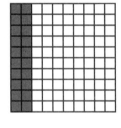

___ ___ ___   ___ ___ ___   ___ ___ ___   ___ ___ ___

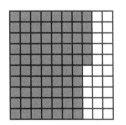
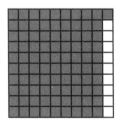
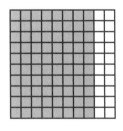

___ ___ ___   ___ ___ ___   ___ ___ ___   ___ ___ ___

Percents and Decimals

Example:

Steps to change a percent to a decimal,
or a decimal to a percent:

PERCENT ⟶ DECIMAL

60% = 60 hundredths = 0.60
3% = 3 hundredths = 0.03
155% = 155 hundredths = 1.55

DECIMAL ⟶ PERCENT

0.35 = 35 hundredths = 35%
0.9 = 90 hundredths = 90%
1.24 = 124 hundredths = 124%

Directions: Write the equivalent decimal or percent.

0.54 =   0.07 =   0.8 =

1.35 =   35% =   125% =

50% =   2% =   2.44 =

0.85 =   23% =   0.5 =

105% =   0.02 =   8% =

10% =   3.00 =   2.08 =

0.05 =   0.89 =   120% =

43% =   3% =   90% =

1.85 =   2.5 =   0.4 =

Presto Change-o!

Directions: Change the following percents to decimals, and the decimals to percents. Remember that percent means "per hundred." The % sign represents hundredths, which is the second decimal place.

1. 45% = _____ **2.** 75% = _____ **3.** 1.11 = _____

4. 0.53 = _____ **5.** 3.1 = _____ **6.** 25% = _____

7. 2.62 = _____ **8.** 14% = _____ **9.** 44% = _____

10. 1% = _____ **11.** 5.32 = _____ **12.** 555% = _____

Directions: Compare using **>**, **<**, or **=**.

13. 15% _____ 0.5

14. 0.04 _____ 2.5%

15. 0.01 _____ 10%

16. 3% _____ 33%

17. 1.3 _____ 13%

18. 0.5 _____ 55%

19. Rudi does magic tricks at the fair. In one night he entertained $\frac{1}{10}$ of the people in attendance. What percent of the people did he entertain?

_____

20. Kerri loves to go on the Tilt-a-Whirl at the fair, but 80% of the time she has to wait in line. What decimal is this?

_____

Lots of Nests

Directions: Write a percent for each fraction. Then, write the word for the percent in the crossword puzzle.

ACROSS

1. There were five squirrels sitting in the nest in the tree. Three-fifths of the squirrels left the nest.

_____

3. After looking carefully at all of the alligator eggs along the river, we think about $\frac{3}{4}$ are ready to hatch.

_____

5. Yellow jackets will protect their nests by stinging anyone who comes near. About $\frac{1}{2}$ of the yellow jackets fly near the nest to guard it.

_____

7. When we disturb a fire ant nest, $\frac{9}{10}$ of the ants race outside to bite their attacker.

_____

DOWN

2. The mother eagle sat on her nest for many days. About $\frac{1}{5}$ of her eggs are ready to hatch.

_____

4. There were many turtle eggs in nests in the woods. About $\frac{16}{20}$ of the eggs were ready to hatch.

_____

6. There are many baby robins sitting on the ground. When a squirrel runs by, $\frac{4}{10}$ of the baby robins fly to their nest.

_____

Simplified Percents

Directions: Write each percent as a fraction in its simplest form.

50% is 50 out of 100.

1. $10\% = \dfrac{1}{10}$ $25\% = $ _____ $95\% = $ _____

2. $80\% = $ _____ $75\% = $ _____ $12\% = $ _____

3. $30\% = $ _____ $18\% = $ _____ $45\% = $ _____ $28\% = $ _____

4. $85\% = $ _____ $96\% = $ _____ $39\% = $ _____ $78\% = $ _____

5. $44\% = $ _____ $65\% = $ _____ $34\% = $ _____ $76\% = $ _____

6. $88\% = $ _____ $56\% = $ _____ $24\% = $ _____ $63\% = $ _____

7. $11\% = $ _____ $42\% = $ _____ $60\% = $ _____ $54\% = $ _____

Directions: Write each fraction as a percent.

8. $\dfrac{1}{2} = $ _____ $\dfrac{3}{10} = $ _____ $\dfrac{2}{5} = $ _____ $\dfrac{1}{10} = $ _____

9. $\dfrac{1}{4} = $ _____ $\dfrac{11}{20} = $ _____ $\dfrac{7}{25} = $ _____ $\dfrac{3}{5} = $ _____

10. $\dfrac{3}{4} = $ _____ $\dfrac{7}{20} = $ _____ $\dfrac{7}{10} = $ _____ $\dfrac{3}{20} = $ _____

11. $\dfrac{9}{10} = $ _____ $\dfrac{4}{5} = $ _____ $\dfrac{10}{25} = $ _____ $\dfrac{11}{100} = $ _____

12. $\dfrac{1}{50} = $ _____ $\dfrac{1}{5} = $ _____ $\dfrac{99}{100} = $ _____ $\dfrac{2}{25} = $ _____

Let's Go Exploring

Directions: Write a decimal for each fraction.

1. 5,496 people are planning our trip. About $\frac{1}{2}$ of those people are building the vehicle.

   _____ = **S**

2. People working on this project live in three cities. Pasadena, California, is home to $\frac{3}{10}$ of the people.

   _____ = **M**

3. Cape Canaveral, Florida, is the town in which $\frac{1}{10}$ of the project workers live.

   _____ = **T**

4. The rest of the exploration crew is from Houston, Texas. That means that $\frac{6}{10}$ live in this southern Texas town.

   _____ = **C**

5. About $\frac{1}{3}$ of the vehicle was made in Detroit, Michigan.

   _____ = **R**

6. Two-thirds of the vehicle was put together in St. Louis, Missouri. Round to the nearest hundredth.

   _____ = **A**

7. When we get the vehicle to its final destination, it can communicate with us only $\frac{3}{4}$ of every day.

   _____ = **O**

Directions: Use the answers and letter clues to write the name of the place we are going.

____ ____   ____ ____ ____ ____
0.1   .75   0.3   .67   .33   0.5

Percents and Fractions

Example:

Steps to change a percent to a fraction,
or a fraction to a percent:

PERCENT ⟶ FRACTION

$67\% = 0.67 = \frac{67}{100}$

$8\% = 0.08 = \frac{8}{100} = \frac{2}{25}$

$125\% = 1.25 = \frac{125}{100} = \frac{5}{4} = 1\frac{1}{4}$

FRACTION ⟶ PERCENT

$\frac{4}{5} = 4 \div 5 = 0.8 = 80\%$

$\frac{1}{3} = 1 \div 3 = 0.333\ldots = 33.3\%$

$1\frac{1}{2} = \frac{3}{2} = 3 \div 2 = 1.5 = 150\%$

Directions: Match the percent with the fraction in simplest form. Write the letter on the line.

1. _____ 5%   **A.** $\frac{3}{25}$ **B.** $\frac{11}{20}$ 2. _____ 12%

3. _____ 17%   **C.** $\frac{1}{3}$ **D.** $1\frac{1}{5}$ 4. _____ 20%

5. _____ 25%   **E.** $\frac{1}{2}$ **F.** $\frac{5}{6}$ 6. _____ 33.3%

7. _____ 48%   **G.** $\frac{1}{5}$ **H.** $\frac{1}{20}$ 8. _____ 50%

9. _____ 55%   **I.** $\frac{7}{10}$ **J.** $\frac{47}{50}$ 10. _____ 70%

11. _____ 75%   **K.** $\frac{1}{4}$ **L.** $1\frac{11}{25}$ 12. _____ 83.3%

13. _____ 94%   **M.** $\frac{17}{100}$ **N.** $\frac{3}{4}$ 14. _____ 120%

15. _____ 144%   **O.** $\frac{12}{25}$

Percent of a Number

Example:

Find 30% of 12.

Method 1
Use a fraction.

Method 2
Use a decimal.

$$\frac{30}{100} \times 12 = \frac{360}{100} = \frac{36}{10} = \frac{18}{5} = 3\frac{3}{5}$$ $$0.3 \times 12 = 3.6$$

30% of 12 is $3\frac{3}{5}$ or 3.6.

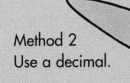

Directions: Find 25% of: Find 4% of: Find 60% of:

16 _____	10 _____	15 _____
20 _____	96 _____	60 _____
64 _____	150 _____	100 _____
140 _____	200 _____	125 _____
10 _____	20 _____	7 _____
35 _____	35 _____	32 _____
120 _____	90 _____	110 _____
630 _____	140 _____	297 _____

Abstract Art

Directions: The grid below contains 100 squares. Each square represents 0.01 or $\frac{1}{100}$ or 1% of all the squares. Use the table below to complete and color in the grid to achieve your own unique design.

Directions: Fill in the table below with all missing amounts.

Color	Fraction	Decimal	Percent	No. of Squares
Blue	$\frac{14}{100}$	0.14	14%	14
Purple				8
Red		0.12		
Yellow	$\frac{26}{100}$			
Green				18
Orange			22%	

Wacky Expressions

Directions: Turn these circles into expressive faces by drawing the correct features on the circles. Match the fraction under each circle with the correct decimal, reduced fraction, and percent below.

1.

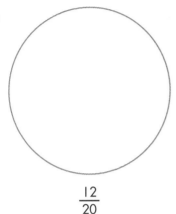

$$\frac{12}{20}$$

2.

$$\frac{75}{100}$$

3.

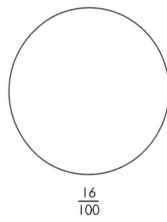

$$\frac{16}{100}$$

4.

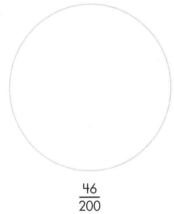

$$\frac{46}{200}$$

5.

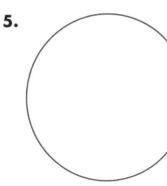

$$\frac{85}{100}$$

6.

$$\frac{4}{100}$$

Eyes	• • $\frac{3}{4}$	⌢ ⌢ 0.6	◗ ◖ 0.04	⬯ ⬯ 16%	ˆ ˆ 0.23	☼ ☼ 85%
Mouths	‿ $\frac{3}{5}$	● $\frac{23}{100}$	⌣ 0.16	∿ 4%	— 75%	⬬ 0.85
Noses	∠ $\frac{17}{20}$	○ $\frac{4}{25}$	⌡ 60%	⌡⁙ 23%	☉ 0.75	△ $\frac{1}{25}$

 Master Math: Introductory Geometry

Flocking Together

Directions: In Australia, huge trees are filled with birds at sunset. Although it can be hard to see these birds at first, you can always hear them! Write a decimal and a percent for each fraction.

1. Of the parrots in the tree, $\frac{8}{12}$ were green. Round to the nearest hundredth.

   _____

2. Four-twelfths of the parrots in the tree were blue.

   _____

3. Five flocks of cockatoos landed in the tree just as the sun set. Four-fifths of these birds were white with yellow crests on their heads.

   _____

4. Three-fifths of the pink cockatoos were less than two years old.

   _____

5. Of the black cockatoos in the tree, $\frac{3}{4}$ sat at the top of the tree.

   _____

6. Five twenty-fifths of the black cockatoos watch the skies for danger.

   _____

7. When the sun rises, $\frac{2}{5}$ of the birds in the tree fly away looking for food.

   _____

Many Names—One Amount

Directions: Complete the table.

	Decimal	Simplest Form Fraction	Percent
1.	0.35		
2.		$\frac{3}{4}$	
3.			50%
4.		$\frac{1}{5}$	
5.	0.04		
6.		$\frac{13}{20}$	
7.			100%
8.			25%
9.	1.50		
10.	0.8		
11.		$\frac{13}{50}$	
12.			1%
13.	0.98		
14.		$\frac{9}{25}$	
15.			13%

Master Math: Introductory Geometry

Ratios

A **ratio** compares two numbers.

Example:

Directions: Put 10 pennies and 10 nickels in a bag. Without looking, pull out a small handful of coins. Draw the coins in a box below. Write each ratio. Return the coins to the bag and repeat 4 more times. The first example is shown.

pennies to nickels _3:5_ coins to pennies _8:3_ nickels to pennies _5:3_ nickels to coins _5:8_ pennies to coins _3:8_ coins to nickels _8:5_	pennies to nickels _____ coins to pennies _____ nickels to pennies _____ nickels to coins _____ pennies to coins _____ coins to nickels _____
pennies to nickels _____ coins to pennies _____ nickels to pennies _____ nickels to coins _____ pennies to coins _____ coins to nickels _____	pennies to nickels _____ coins to pennies _____ nickels to pennies _____ nickels to coins _____ pennies to coins _____ coins to nickels _____
pennies to nickels _____ coins to pennies _____ nickels to pennies _____ nickels to coins _____ pennies to coins _____ coins to nickels _____	pennies to nickels _____ coins to pennies _____ nickels to pennies _____ nickels to coins _____ pennies to coins _____ coins to nickels _____

Ratio, Ratio, Ratio

Directions: Write three ways to express each ratio.

1.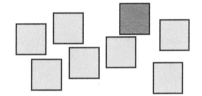

      3 to 4 _____   _____   _____

      3:4 _____   _____   _____

      $\frac{3}{4}$ _____   _____   _____

2.

_____   _____   _____

_____   _____   _____

_____   _____   _____

3.

_____   _____   _____

_____   _____   _____

_____   _____   _____

4.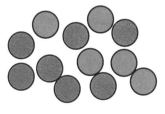

2 2 2 2 3
2 2 2 2 3
2 2 2 2 3

_____   _____   _____

_____   _____   _____

_____   _____   _____

Working With Ratios

A ratio is a comparison of two numbers. There are several ways to express a ratio.

| 12 out of 20 | 12 to 20 | 12:20 | $\frac{12}{20} = \frac{3}{5}$ |

Directions: Fill in the blank spaces on the table below.

	Verbal description	a to b	a:b	$\frac{a}{b}$ (simplified)
1.	10 out of 15	10 to 15	10:15	$\frac{2}{3}$
2.	6 out of 20			
3.		9 to 10		
4.			5:50	
5.	16 out of 48			
6.				$\frac{3}{8}$
7.		13 to 52		
8.	18 out of 90			
9.			15:45	
10.	3 out of 7			
11.				$\frac{4}{11}$
12.	105 out of 150			
13.		8 to 12		

Proportions

Another way of writing a ratio is $\frac{3}{7}$ as a fraction. 3:7 is the same as $\frac{3}{7}$. Remember what you have learned about cross multiplication.
$$\frac{1}{2} \times \frac{4}{8}$$

Because the products of cross multiplication are the same, the fractions are equivalent. When two ratios or fractions are equivalent, they form a **proportion**.

Example:

Steps to find an unknown term of a proportion:

Lisa uses 2 pots to plant 8 seeds.
How many pots will she need to plant 24 seeds?

1. Write a proportion. $\frac{2 \text{ pots}}{8 \text{ seeds}} = \frac{n \text{ pots}}{24 \text{ seeds}}$

2. Cross multiply. $\frac{2}{8} \times \frac{n}{24}$

$8 \times n = 48$
$n = 6$ (Divide both sides of the proportion by 8.)
Lisa needs 6 pots to plant 24 seeds.

Directions: If the ratios form a proportion, write **yes** on the line. If not, write **no**.

$\frac{4}{5} = \frac{24}{30}$ _____ $\frac{1}{2} = \frac{36}{72}$ _____ $\frac{3}{7} = \frac{20}{35}$ _____ $\frac{1}{23} = \frac{8}{184}$ _____

$\frac{6}{13} = \frac{75}{156}$ _____ $\frac{9}{5} = \frac{171}{95}$ _____ $\frac{4}{21} = \frac{40}{210}$ _____ $\frac{11}{12} = \frac{154}{168}$ _____

Directions: Find the unknown term in each of these proportions.

$\frac{4}{5} = \frac{n}{15}$ _____ $\frac{n}{104} = \frac{5}{13}$ _____ $\frac{5}{6} = \frac{45}{n}$ _____

Master Math: Introductory Geometry

Ratio and Proportion

A proportion shows that two ratios are equal.	Use cross products to find the missing number in a proportion.

$$\frac{4}{12} = \frac{1}{3}$$

4 out of 12 counters are shaded.
1 out of 3 rows is shaded.

$$\frac{4}{12} \diagdown \frac{1}{n}$$

$$4n = 12$$
$$n = 3$$

Directions: Solve each proportion. You may use a calculator to help you.

1. $\frac{n}{4} = \frac{6}{8}$ $\frac{n}{6} = \frac{15}{12}$ $\frac{15}{20} = \frac{n}{4}$

n = _____   n = _____   n = _____

2. $\frac{8}{36} = \frac{2}{n}$ $\frac{15}{12} = \frac{n}{4}$ $\frac{7}{8} = \frac{n}{56}$

n = _____   n = _____   n = _____

3. $\frac{7}{9} = \frac{63}{n}$ $\frac{n}{3} = \frac{15}{45}$ $\frac{14}{8} = \frac{42}{n}$

n = _____   n = _____   n = _____

4. $\frac{4}{n} = \frac{8}{3}$ $\frac{2}{n} = \frac{5}{7.5}$ $\frac{n}{39} = \frac{10}{13}$

n = _____   n = _____   n = _____

5. $\frac{7}{6} = \frac{56}{n}$ $\frac{5}{3} = \frac{105}{n}$ $\frac{n}{4.2} = \frac{1}{3}$

n = _____   n = _____   n = _____

What Are the Chances?

Probability is the chance that something will happen.

Example:

This spinner has 8 equal-sized spaces. What is the probability, or chance, that a person would spin:

Blue? $\frac{4}{8}$ or 4:8, because 4 of 8 sections are blue.

Red? $\frac{1}{8}$ or 1:8, because 1 of 8 sections is red.

Yellow? $\frac{2}{8}$ or 2:8, because 2 of 8 sections are yellow.

Green? $\frac{1}{8}$ or 1:8, because 1 of 8 sections is green.

Directions: Use the spinner to the right to answer the questions.

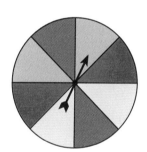

1. What is the probability of spinning blue? _____

2. What is the probability of spinning yellow? _____

3. What is the probability of spinning green? _____

4. What is the probability of spinning yellow or red? _____

Directions: Use the spinner to the right to answer the questions.

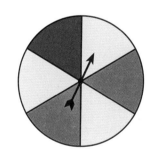

1. What is the probability of spinning purple? _____

2. What is the probability of spinning orange? _____

3. What is the probability of spinning yellow? _____

4. What is the probability of spinning yellow, orange, or purple? _____

Directions: Use the spinner to the right to answer the questions.

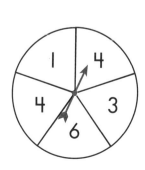

1. What is the probability of spinning a 4? _____

2. What is the probability of spinning a 1? _____

3. What is the probability of spinning a 3? _____

4. What is the probability of spinning 3, 4, or 6? _____

Photo Safari

Directions: The students at Carver School are going to take pictures of wildlife. Help the students find the probability. Write each fraction. Reduce the fraction to its lowest terms, if necessary.

1. The first trip was to the woods. Stella startled a group of 3 raccoons, 2 skunks, 4 opossums, and 1 weasel. She took a picture quickly without really looking.

    What is the probability Stella photographed a weasel? _____

    What is the probability she photographed a skunk? _____

    What is the probability she photographed an opossum? _____

    What is the probability she photographed a raccoon? _____

2. Livingston doesn't know it, but he's surrounded by 6 flying squirrels, 4 bats, 7 owls, and 3 night herons.

    If he looks up, what is the probability he will see an owl? _____

    What is the probability he will see a flying squirrel? _____

    What is the probability he will see a bat? _____

    What is the probability he will see a night heron? _____

3. Jasmin likes animals that crawl. In the soil where she is waiting, there are 3 night crawlers, 2 centipedes, 1 ant lion, and 4 beetles.

    What is the probability she will see an ant lion? _____

    What is the probability she will see a beetle? _____

    What is the probability she will see a centipede? _____

    What is the probability she will see a night crawler? _____

4. The next trip the students took was to the desert. More animals roam the desert at night, when it is cooler than during the daytime. Lamar rests on a rock. Nearby are 2 sidewinders, 5 scorpions, 4 kangaroo rats, and 3 owls.

    What is the probability he will see a scorpion? _____

    What is the probability he will see a sidewinder? _____

    What is the probability he will see an owl? _____

    What is the probability he will see a kangaroo rat? _____

Likely and Unlikely

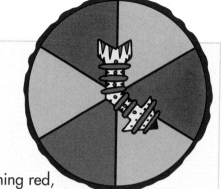

The probability of an event happening can be written as a fraction between 0 and 1.

Example:

Certain if the probability is 1.

The probability of spinning red, blue, or green is $\frac{6}{6}$ or 1.

More likely if its probability is greater than another.

It is more likely to spin green ($\frac{3}{6}$) than red ($\frac{2}{6}$).

Less likely if its probability is less than another.

It is less likely to spin blue ($\frac{1}{6}$) than red ($\frac{2}{6}$).

Equally likely if the probabilities are the same.

It is equally likely to spin red or blue ($\frac{3}{6}$) or green ($\frac{3}{6}$).

Impossible if the probability is 0.

It is impossible to spin white ($\frac{0}{6} = 0$).

Directions: Look at the spinner. Write the probability for each event below. Write **certain** or **impossible**, where appropriate.

spinning a 6 _____   spinning a 4 _____

spinning a 2 _____   spinning a 4 or 5 _____

spinning an even number _____   spinning a prime number _____

spinning a number < 10 _____   spinning a zero _____

Directions: Look at the spinner to find which is **more likely**, **less likely**, or **equally likely**.

Spinning a 4 is _____ than spinning a 5.

Spinning a 4 is _____ than spinning a 1.

Spinning an even number is _____ than spinning an odd number.

Predicting Outcomes

To find the probability of an outcome, we must find the relative frequency of that outcome. This can be expressed as a ratio:

$$\frac{\textbf{frequency of outcome}}{\textbf{total frequency of all outcomes}}$$

We can also use this equation to predict future outcomes. Simply make an equality with **n** (the frequency) as an unknown number.

For example, if $\frac{12}{50}$ is the probability of having a rainy day out of 50 days, then $\frac{n}{100}$ might be the prediction of having **n** amount of rainy days out of 100 days.

$$\frac{4}{5} = \frac{24}{30}$$

$$n = 24$$

Directions: Solve the probability problems below.

1. If the probability of having rain is $\frac{8}{50}$, meaning that rain had fallen 8 out of the last 50 days, how many days would you expect it to rain out of the next 100?

    _____

2. Explain why using probability may or may not be a good way to predict the weather.

    _____

    _____

3. If 32 out of 36 students pick red as their favorite color, what could you assume about the results of a sampling of 108 students?

    _____

    _____

Playing Games

Directions: Solve the probability problems below.

1. A jar contains 4 blue marbles, 8 red marbles, 2 yellow marbles, and 12 orange marbles. Find the probability of:

    a. P (red or blue marble)   _____

    b. P (orange marble)   _____

    c. P (yellow or orange marble) _____

    d. P (a marble)   _____

    e. P (a green marble)   _____

2. Marty and Chandra have played jacks during recess 18 out of the last 30 days. What is the probability that they will play jacks today?

    _____

3. During indoor recess, Leah, Shalti, and Benny were allowed to play with either the pogo stick, the yo-yo, or the jump rope. In how many different ways can the students be matched to the toys? List them. _____

    _____

4. Fifty students were surveyed. Forty preferred soccer to four-square. Predict how many students out of 200 would prefer soccer.

    _____

5. For being star of the week, Justin may choose to play either jacks, go-fish, or solitaire, and he may choose a snack of popcorn or pretzels. What is the probability he will choose jacks and popcorn?

    _____

Movie Time

Directions: Use the data in the table to make a circle graph.

Movie Viewing Preferences	
Comedy	$\frac{5}{12}$
Drama	$\frac{1}{12}$
Suspense	$\frac{2}{12}$
Science fiction	$\frac{4}{12}$

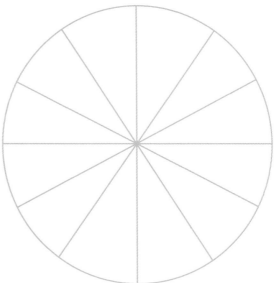

Be sure to color and label each category.

Directions: Use the circle graph to answer the questions. Assume that 120 people took part in the survey.

1. How many people prefer suspense movies?

_____

2. How many people prefer comedies?

_____

3. How many more people chose suspense than drama?

_____

4. Which type of movie was chosen 4 times as often as drama?

_____

5. Which categories were chosen by fewer than 30 people?

_____

6. If 4 more people had chosen suspense instead of comedy, how would the results be changed?

_____

Flying Forks

Directions: Look at a plastic fork. What do you think will happen if you drop the fork—will it land faceup, facedown, or on its side? What is the probability of each position?

PREDICT:

Imagine dropping the fork 50 different times.
Predict how many times the fork will land:

Faceup: _____

Facedown: _____

On its side: _____

EXPERIMENT:

Drop the fork 50 times. Record how many times it lands in each position.

Faceup: _____

Facedown: _____

On its side: _____

ORGANIZE THE DATA:

Graph the results.

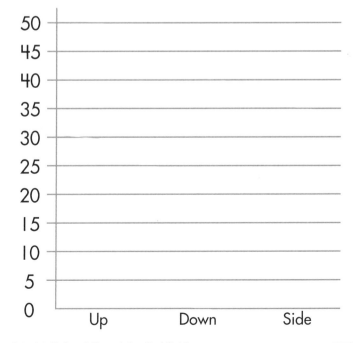

INTERPRET THE DATA:

Explain what the results mean. Why might these results have occurred?

_____

_____

_____

_____

_____

_____

_____

Scores and Statistics

Directions: Rewrite the data in order from least to greatest. Then, find the range, mean, median, and mode. Round to the nearest ten.

1. 79, 90, 85, 66, 77, 77, 91

____ ____ ____ ____ ____ ____ ____

Range: _____   Mean: _____

Median: _____   Mode: _____

2. 86, 96, 59, 74, 59, 82, 70

____ ____ ____ ____ ____ ____ ____

Range: _____   Mean: _____

Median: _____   Mode: _____

3. 83, 90, 54, 77, 54, 86, 72

____ ____ ____ ____ ____ ____ ____

Range: _____   Mean: _____

Median: _____   Mode: _____

4. 72, 65, 36, 56, 87, 97, 65, 58

____ ____ ____ ____ ____ ____ ____ ____

Range: _____   Mean: _____

Median: _____   Mode: _____

5. 82, 57, 46, 67, 89, 97, 67, 55

____ ____ ____ ____ ____ ____ ____ ____

Range: _____   Mean: _____

Median: _____   Mode: _____

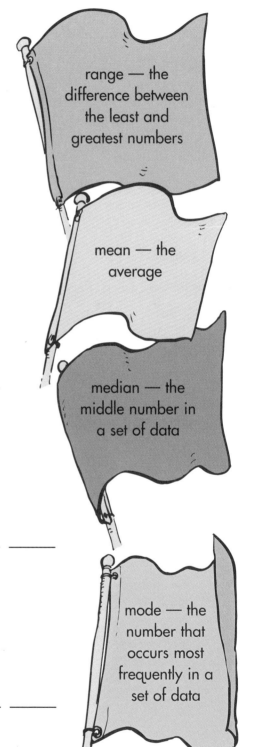

range — the difference between the least and greatest numbers

mean — the average

median — the middle number in a set of data

mode — the number that occurs most frequently in a set of data

Graphing Test Results

Directions: Use the data in the table to make a bar graph.

Sam's Test Score Averages	
English	95
Math	90
Social Studies	60
Science	80
Spanish	75
Health	70

Be sure your graph has a title, headings, numbers, and bars.

Directions: Use the graph to answer the questions.

1. In which subject does Sam have the lowest average?

_____

2. In which subject does Sam have the highest average?

_____

3. How many points must Sam gain in order to have an average of 70 in Social Studies?

_____

4. Sam's average in math is 10 points higher than what subject area?

_____

5. Sam has a 5-point bonus coupon that he can use to bring one grade up. Tell which subject he should choose. Explain your answer.

_____

_____

69 *Master Math: Introductory Geometry*

Name _____

What's the Vote?

Directions: Alyson's class is interested in growing a flower garden for the whole school to enjoy. To collect data on flower preferences, they surveyed the students in the school. Out of an enrollment of 435, the following resulted.

Favorite Flowers	
Type of Flowers	**Number of Votes**
Black-Eyed Susan	57
Lavender	63
Iris	32
Tulip	78
Hollyhock	7
Daffodil	53
Daisy	84

Directions: Based on the data, answer the questions below.

1. List the flowers in order from the least popular to the most popular.

_____

_____

2. Based on the data, which 5 flowers should the class plant?

_____

_____

3. Which flower should definitely not be planted? _____

4. Do the number of votes justify planting a garden? _____

Why? _____

_____

5. What is the mean? _____

6. What is the mode? _____

7. What is the median? _____

8. What is the range? _____

Lines

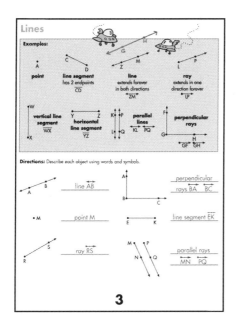

Examples:

point • A

line segment — has 2 endpoints $\overline{CD}$

line — extends forever in both directions $\overleftrightarrow{ZM}$

ray — extends in one direction forever $\overrightarrow{LP}$

vertical line segment $\overline{WX}$

horizontal line segment $\overline{YZ}$

parallel lines $\overline{KL}$ $\overline{PQ}$

perpendicular rays $\overrightarrow{GF}$ $\overrightarrow{GH}$

Directions: Describe each object using words and symbols.

line AB

perpendicular rays BA BC

point M

line segment EK

ray RS

parallel rays MN PQ

3

What's Your Angle?

Angles can be classified into 4 groups. They are classified by their angle measures.

An **acute angle** is less than 90°.

A **right angle** equals exactly 90°.

An **obtuse angle** is between 90° and 180°.

A **straight angle** equals exactly 180°.

Directions: Classify each angle as acute, right, obtuse, or straight.

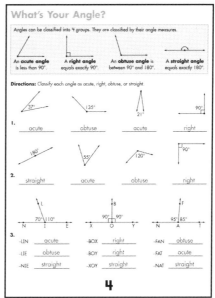

1. 37° acute | 135° obtuse | 21° acute | 90° right

2. 180° straight | 55° acute | 120° obtuse | 90° right

3.
∠LIN acute | ∠BOX right | ∠FAN obtuse
∠LIE obtuse | ∠BOY right | ∠FAT acute
∠NIE straight | ∠XOY straight | ∠NAT straight

4

Sail Away With Angles

Directions: Look at each triangle. Use the measurements given to write the kind of triangle on the line (**right**, **acute**, or **obtuse**). Then, find the missing angle. Put the corresponding letter of the angle above its measurement at the bottom of the page to answer the riddle.

Example: a = 180° − (90° + 42°) = 48°   Right

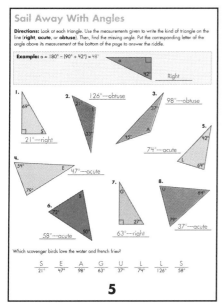

1. 69° 21°—right
2. 126°—obtuse
3. 98°—obtuse
   74°—acute
4. 54° 47°—acute
5. 42°
6. 42° 58°—acute
7. 63°—right
8. 64° 37°—acute

Which scavenger birds love the water and french fries?

S E A G U L L S
21° 47° 98° 63° 37° 74° 126° 58°

5

Star Light, Star Bright

A man was driving a black truck. His lights were not on. The moon was not out. A lady was crossing the street. How did the man see her?

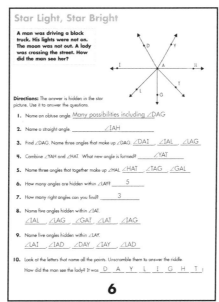

Directions: The answer is hidden in the star picture. Use it to answer the questions.

1. Name an obtuse angle. Many possibilities including ∠DAG
2. Name a straight angle. ∠IAH
3. Find ∠DAG. Name three angles that make up ∠DAG. ∠DAI ∠IAL ∠LAG
4. Combine ∠YAH and ∠HAT. What new angle is formed? ∠YAT
5. Name three angles that together make up ∠HAL. ∠HAT ∠TAG ∠GAL
6. How many angles are hidden within ∠LAY? 5
7. How many right angles can you find? 3
8. Name five angles hidden within ∠IAT.
   ∠IAL ∠LAG ∠GAT ∠LAT ∠IAG
9. Name five angles hidden within ∠LAY.
   ∠LAI ∠IAD ∠DAY ∠IAY ∠LAD
10. Look at the letters that name all the points. Unscramble them to answer the riddle. How did the man see the lady? It was D A Y L I G H T !

6

Mirror, Mirror

A **line of symmetry** divides a shape into two matching halves. A shape can have any number of lines of symmetry.

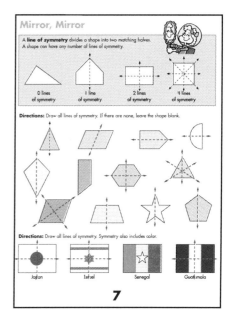

0 lines of symmetry | 1 line of symmetry | 2 lines of symmetry | 4 lines of symmetry

Directions: Draw all lines of symmetry. If there are none, leave the shape blank.

Directions: Draw all lines of symmetry. Symmetry also includes color.

Japan | Israel | Senegal | Guatemala

7

Alike and Different

Shapes are **congruent** if they are exactly the same size and shape.

congruent

Shapes are **similar** if they are about the same relative size.

similar

Directions: Label the shapes in each pair as congruent, similar, or neither.

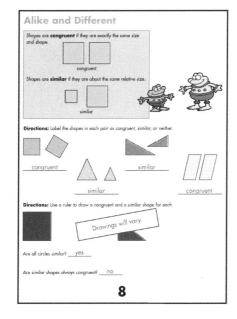

congruent | similar
similar | congruent

Directions: Use a ruler to draw a congruent and a similar shape for each.

Drawings will vary.

Are all circles similar? yes

Are similar shapes always congruent? no

8

Classifying Triangles by Their Sides

Triangles can be classified by the lengths of their sides.

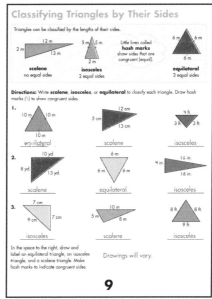

scalene — no equal sides
Little lines called **hash marks** show sides that are congruent (equal).
isosceles — 2 equal sides
equilateral — 3 equal sides

Directions: Write **scalene**, **isosceles**, or **equilateral** to classify each triangle. Draw hash marks (\\) to show congruent sides.

1. 10 m 10 m 10 m — equilateral | 12 cm 5 cm 13 cm — scalene | 4 ft. 3 ft. 3 ft. — isosceles
2. 10 yd. 8 yd. 13 yd. — scalene | 6 m 6 m 6 m — equilateral | 16 in. 4 in. 16 in. — isosceles
3. 7 cm 9 cm 7 cm — isosceles | 10 m 5 m 8 m — scalene | 8 ft. 8 ft. 9 ft. — isosceles

In the space to the right, draw and label an equilateral triangle, an isosceles triangle, and a scalene triangle. Make hash marks to indicate congruent sides.

Drawings will vary.

9

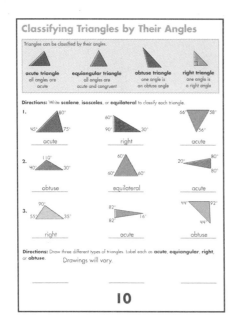
Perimeter

The **perimeter** is the distance around a shape.

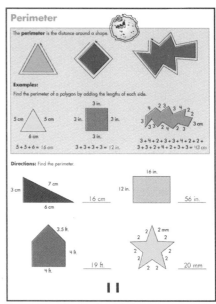

Examples:
Find the perimeter of a polygon by adding the lengths of each side.

5 cm   5 cm
6 cm
5 + 5 + 6 = 16 cm

3 in.
3 in.   3 in.
3 in.
3 + 3 + 3 + 3 = 12 in.

4 + 2 + 3 + 3 + 4 + 2 + 3 + 3 + 2 + 4 + 2 + 3 + 3 = 43 cm

Directions: Find the perimeter.

3 cm   7 cm
6 cm
16 cm

16 in.
12 in.
56 in.

3.5 ft.
4 ft.
4 ft.
19 ft.

2 mm   2
2   2
2   2
20 mm

11

Circles

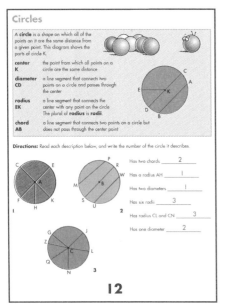

A **circle** is a shape on which all of the points on it are the same distance from a given point. This diagram shows the parts of circle K.

center K the point from which all points on a circle are the same distance

diameter CD a line segment that connects two points on a circle and passes through the center

radius EK a line segment that connects the center with any point on the circle. The plural of **radius** is **radii.**

chord AB a line segment that connects two points on a circle but does not pass through the center point

Directions: Read each description below, and write the number of the circle it describes.

Has two chords ___2___

Has a radius AH ___1___

Has two diameters ___1___

Has six radii ___3___

Has radius CL and CN ___3___

Has one diameter ___2___

12

The Circle Game

The perimeter of a circle is called the **circumference.** There is a formula for finding the circumference of a circle. The formula uses this special number, **3.14.** We call this number **pi** (π). To find the circumference of a circle, use this formula:

Circumference = π × diameter
Circumference = πd
or
Circumference = π × 2 × radius
Circumference = 2πr

Examples:
C = πd   C = 2πr
C = 3.14 × 4   C = 2 × 3.14 × 2
C = 12.56   C = 12.56

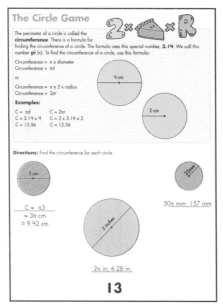

4 cm

2 cm

Directions: Find the circumference for each circle.

3 cm

2 cm
50π mm; 157 mm

C = π3
 = 3π cm
 ≈ 9.42 cm

2 inches

2π in; 6.28 in.

13

Waterlogged

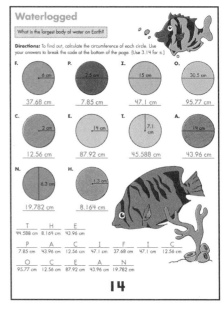

What is the largest body of water on Earth?

Directions: To find out, calculate the circumference of each circle. Use your answers to break the code at the bottom of the page. (Use 3.14 for π.)

F. 6 cm — 37.68 cm

P. 2.5 cm — 7.85 cm

I. 15 cm — 47.1 cm

O. 30.5 cm — 95.77 cm

C. 2 cm — 12.56 cm

E. 14 cm — 87.92 cm

T. 7.1 cm — 45.588 cm

A. 14 cm — 43.96 cm

N. 6.3 cm — 19.782 cm

H. 1.3 cm — 8.164 cm

T	H	E
44.588 cm	8.164 cm	43.96 cm

P	A	C	I	F	I	C
7.85 cm	43.96 cm	12.56 cm	47.1 cm	37.68 cm	47.1 cm	12.56 cm

O	C	E	A	N
95.77 cm	12.56 cm	87.92 cm	43.96 cm	19.782 cm

14

Exploring Circumference and Diameter

Study the definitions in the term box and look closely at the circle to understand and answer the questions below.

Terms

Circumference: the distance around a circle

Diameter: a segment connecting two points on a circle and going through the center of the circle

Radius: a line segment connecting the center of a circle to any point on the circle

Central Angle: an angle whose vertex is at the center of a circle

Center: a point such that every point on the circle is the same distance from it

Chord: any line segment that connects two points on a circle

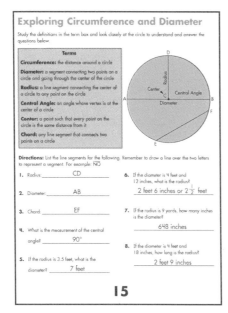

Directions: List the line segments for the following. Remember to draw a line over the two letters to represent a segment. For example: NO

1. Radius: ___CD___

2. Diameter: ___AB___

3. Chord: ___EF___

4. What is the measurement of the central angle? ___90°___

5. If the radius is 3.5 feet, what is the diameter? ___7 feet___

6. If the diameter is 4 feet and 12 inches, what is the radius? ___2 feet 6 inches or 2½ feet___

7. If the radius is 9 yards, how many inches is the diameter? ___648 inches___

8. If the diameter is 4 feet and 18 inches, how long is the radius? ___2 feet 9 inches___

15

Formula One

To find the **area** of a square or rectangle, multiply the length by the width.

Example:

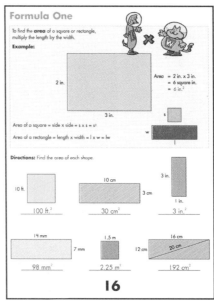

2 in.
3 in.

Area = 2 in. × 3 in.
 = 6 square in.
 = 6 in.²

s

w
l

Area of a square = side × side = s × s = s²

Area of a rectangle = length × width = l × w = lw

Directions: Find the area of each shape.

10 ft.
100 ft.²

10 cm
3 cm
30 cm²

3 in.
1 in.
3 in.²

14 mm
7 mm
98 mm²

1.5 m
2.25 m²

16 cm
12 cm   20 cm
192 cm²

16

Area of Rectangles and Squares

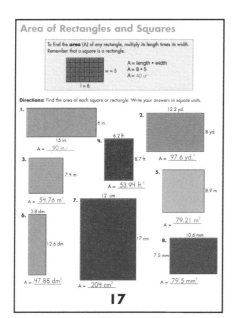

To find the **area** (A) of any rectangle, multiply its length times its width. Remember that a square is a rectangle.

$$A = length \cdot width$$
$$A = 8 \cdot 5$$
$$A = 40 \, u^2$$

w = 5   l = 8

Directions: Find the area of each square or rectangle. Write your answers in square units.

1. 6 in. / 15 in. A = __90 in.²__
2. 12.2 yd. / 8 yd. A = __97.6 yd.²__
4. 6.2 ft. / 8.7 ft. A = __53.94 ft.²__
3. 7.4 m A = __54.76 m²__
5. 8.9 m A = __79.21 m³__
6. 3.8 dm / 12.6 dm A = __47.88 dm²__
7. 12 cm / 17 cm A = __204 cm²__
8. 10.6 mm / 7.5 mm A = __79.5 mm²__

17

An A-peel-ing Riddle

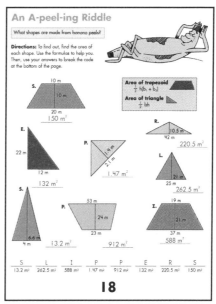

What shapes are made from banana peels?

Directions: To find out, find the area of each shape. Use the formulas to help you. Then, use your answers to break the code at the bottom of the page.

Area of trapezoid: ½ h(b₁ + b₂)
Area of triangle: ½ bh

S. 10 m / 10 m / 20 m __150 m²__
E. 22 m / 12 m __132 m²__
P. 1.4 m / 2.1 m __1.47 m²__
R. 10.5 m / 42 m __220.5 m²__
L. 21 m / 25 m __262.5 m²__
S. 6.6 m / 4 m __13.2 m²__
P. 53 m / 24 m / 23 m __912 m²__
I. 19 m / 21 m / 37 m __588 m²__

S __13.2 m²__ L __262.5 m²__ I __588 m²__ P __1.47 m²__ P __912 m²__ E __132 m²__ R __220.5 m²__ S __150 m²__

18

Area

Triangle:	area = ½ base x height
Rectangle/Square:	area = base x height
Parallelogram:	area = base x height
Trapezoid:	area = ½ height (base + base)

Directions: Find the area of the polygonal regions below. Express in square units.

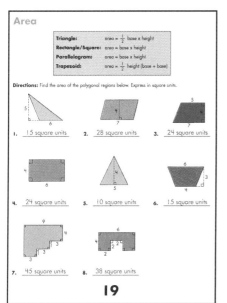

1. __15 square units__
2. __28 square units__
3. __24 square units__
4. __24 square units__
5. __10 square units__
6. __15 square units__
7. __45 square units__
8. __38 square units__

19

Compound Figures

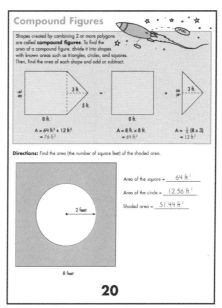

Shapes created by combining 2 or more polygons are called **compound figures**. To find the area of a compound figure, divide it into shapes with known areas such as triangles, circles, and squares. Then, find the area of each shape and add or subtract.

8 ft. / 3 ft. / 5 ft.
A = 64 ft² + 12 ft² = 76 ft²
= 8 ft. x 8 ft. = 64 ft²
+ A = ½ (8 x 3) = 12 ft²

Directions: Find the area (the number of square feet) of the shaded area.

2 feet / 8 feet

Area of the square = __64 ft.²__
Area of the circle = __12.56 ft.²__
Shaded area = __51.44 ft.²__

20

Area of Parallelograms

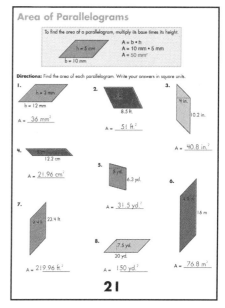

To find the area of a parallelogram, multiply its base times its height.

A = b • h
A = 10 mm • 5 mm
A = 50 mm²

h = 5 mm / b = 10 mm

Directions: Find the area of each parallelogram. Write your answers in square units.

1. h = 3 mm / b = 12 mm A = __36 mm²__
2. 8.5 ft. A = __51 ft.²__
3. 4 in. / 10.2 in. A = __40.8 in.²__
4. 12.2 cm A = __21.96 cm²__
5. 5 yd. / 6.3 yd. A = __31.5 yd.²__
6. 4.8 m / 16 m A = __76.8 m²__
7. 9.4 ft. / 23.4 ft. A = __219.96 ft.²__
8. 7.5 yd. / 20 yd. A = __150 yd.²__

21

Area of Trapezoids

To find the area of a trapezoid, use the formula ½ (base₁ + base₂) • height.

A = ½ (b₁ + b₂) • h
A = ½ (10 + 12) • 6
A = ½ (22 • 6)
A = 66 ft.²

b₁ = 10 ft. / h = 6 ft. / b₂ = 12 ft.

Directions: Write an equation using the formula ½ (b₁ + b₂) • h. Use it to find the area of each trapezoid. Work on scratch paper. Write your answers in square units.

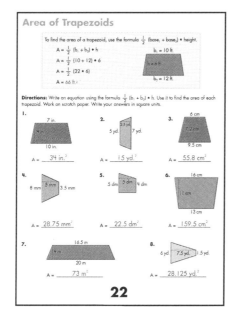

1. 7 in. / 4 in. / 10 in. A = __34 in.²__
2. 2.5 yd. / 5 yd. / 7 yd. A = __15 yd.²__
3. 6 cm / 7.2 cm / 9.5 cm A = __55.8 cm²__
4. 8 mm / 5 mm / 3.5 mm A = __28.75 mm²__
5. 5 dm / 5 dm / 4 dm A = __22.5 dm²__
6. 16 cm / 11 cm / 13 cm A = __159.5 cm²__
7. 16.5 m / 4 m / 20 m A = __73 m²__
8. 6 yd. / 7.5 yd. / 1.5 yd. A = __28.125 yd.²__

22

Mad Measurements

What can be measured but has no length, width, or thickness?

Directions: To find out, calculate the missing measurements below. Write the corresponding letters with the answers at the bottom of the page. All measurements are cm.

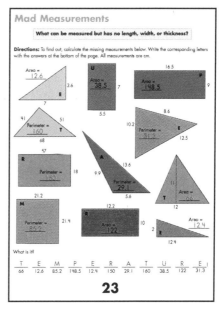

E. Area = __12.6__ / 3.6 / 7
U. Area = __38.5__ / 5.5 / 7
P. 16.5 / Area = __148.5__ / 9
T. Perimeter = __160__ / 41 / 51 / 68
E. 8.6 / 10.2 / Perimeter = __31.2__ / 12.5
R. 57 / Perimeter = __150__ / 18 / 21.2
A. 13.6 / 9.9 / Perimeter = __29.1__ / 5.6
T. (?) / Area = __66__ / 12
M. Perimeter = __85.2__ / 21.4
R. 12.2 / Area = __122__ / 10
E. 2 / Area = __12.4__ / 12.4

What is it?

T __66__ E __12.6__ M __85.2__ P __148.5__ E __12.4__ R __150__ A __29.1__ T __160__ U __38.5__ R __122__ E __31.3__

23

73

To the Edge

Polyhedra can be described by the number of faces, edges, and vertices (a vertex is where three edges meet) they have.

A cube has 6 faces, 8 vertices, and 12 edges.

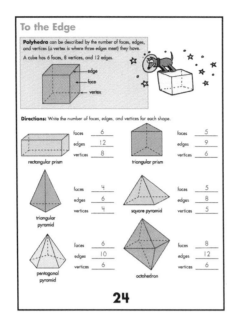

Directions: Write the number of faces, edges, and vertices for each shape.

rectangular prism — faces 6, edges 12, vertices 8

triangular prism — faces 5, edges 9, vertices 6

triangular pyramid — faces 4, edges 6, vertices 4

square pyramid — faces 5, edges 8, vertices 5

pentagonal pyramid — faces 6, edges 10, vertices 6

octahedron — faces 8, edges 12, vertices 6

24

Pump Up the Volume!

The **volume** of a 3-D shape is the amount of space it occupies. Volume is measured in cubic units, such as cubic centimeters (cm³) or cubic inches (in.³).

Imagine a box filled with unit cubes. The number of cubes is the volume of the box.

The box has a volume of 16 cubic units.

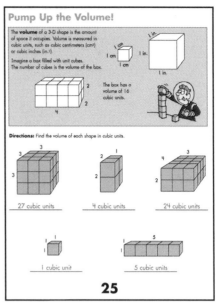

Directions: Find the volume of each shape in cubic units.

27 cubic units   4 cubic units   24 cubic units

1 cubic unit   5 cubic units

25

How Much Does It Hold?

Directions: Find the volume of each figure. Use the formula
Volume = length x width x height. You may use a calculator if you have one.

Remember to write your answer in cubic units.

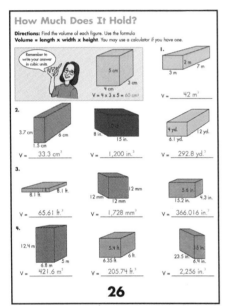

V = 4 x 3 x 5 = 60 cm³

1. V = ___ 42 m³

2. V = 33.3 cm³   V = 1,200 in.³   V = 292.8 yd.³

3. V = 65.61 ft.³   V = 1,728 mm³   V = 366.016 in.³

4. V = 421.6 m³   V = 205.74 ft.³   V = 2,256 in.³

26

Volume Variation

To find the volume of a **cylinder**, a **pyramid**, and a **sphere**, follow these directions:

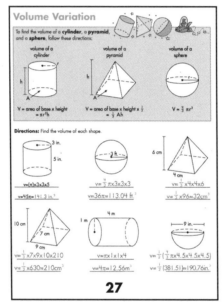

volume of a cylinder
V = area of base x height
= πr²h

volume of a pyramid
V = area of base x height x ⅓
= ⅓ Ah

volume of a sphere
V = ⁴⁄₃ πr³

Directions: Find the volume of each shape.

v=(π)x3x3x5
v=45π≈141.3 in.³

v=⁴⁄₃ πx3x3x3
v=36π≈113.04 in.³

v=⅓x4x4x6
v=⅓x96=32cm³

v=⅓x7x9x10x210
v=⅓x630≈210cm³

v=πx1x1x4
v=4π≈12.56in.³

v=½(⁴⁄₃πx4.5x4.5x4.5)
v=½(381.51)≈190.76in.³

27

Graphing in Four Quadrants

To graph an ordered pair, start at the origin, (0, 0). Move **x** units right or left. Then, move **y** units up or down.

The ★ is at point (⁻1,⁻4). Since both numbers are negative (⁻), it is in Quadrant III.

To plot this point, you would
Start at the origin.
Move 1 unit to the left.
Move 4 units down.

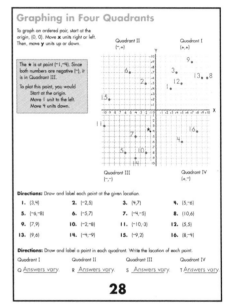

Quadrant II (⁻,+)   Quadrant I (+,+)
Quadrant III (⁻,⁻)   Quadrant IV (+,⁻)

Directions: Draw and label each point at the given location.

1. (3,4)   2. (⁻2,5)   3. (4,7)   4. (5,⁻6)
5. (⁻6,⁻8)   6. (⁻5,7)   7. (⁻4,⁻5)   8. (10,6)
9. (7,9)   10. (⁻2,⁻8)   11. (⁻10,3)   12. (5,5)
13. (9,6)   14. (⁻4,⁻9)   15. (⁻9,2)   16. (8,⁻4)

Directions: Draw and label a point in each quadrant. Write the location of each point.

Quadrant I — Q Answers vary.
Quadrant II — R Answers vary.
Quadrant III — S Answers vary.
Quadrant IV — T Answers vary.

28

Decimal Drawings

Decimals represent numbers that include a part of a whole. With decimals, the part that is less than 1 is always separated into 10, or a power of 10, parts.

one — 1
one tenth — 0.1
one hundredth — 0.01

Examples:
0.2   0.75   1.00

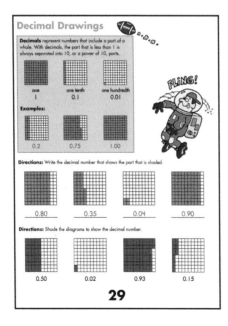

FLING!

Directions: Write the decimal number that shows the part that is shaded.

0.80   0.35   0.04   0.90

Directions: Shade the diagrams to show the decimal number.

0.50   0.02   0.93   0.15

29

That's the Point

When writing a decimal, place the decimal point between the ones column and the tenths column. Here are some place values to the right and left of the decimal point.

| hundreds | tens | ones | . | tenths | hundredths | thousandths |

Steps:
1. Read the whole number.
2. Say the word "and" or "point."
3. Read the number after the decimal point.
4. Say the decimal place of the last digit to the right.

Examples:
45.91 is read "forty-five and ninety-one hundredths"
222.1 is read "two hundred twenty-two point one"
10.004 is read "ten and four thousandths"

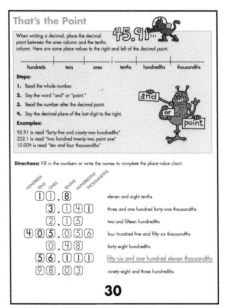

45.91

and
or
point

Directions: Fill in the numbers or write the names to complete the place-value chart.

HUNDREDS	TENS	ONES	TENTHS	HUNDREDTHS	THOUSANDTHS	
1	1	.	8			eleven and eight tenths
	3	.	1	4	1	three and one hundred forty-one thousandths
	2	.	1	5		two and fifteen hundredths
4	0	5	.	0	5	6	four hundred five and fifty-six thousandths
	0	.	4	8		forty-eight hundredths
5	6	.	1	1	1	fifty-six and one hundred eleven thousandths
9	8	.	0	3		ninety-eight and three hundredths

30

April Showers

Comparing and ordering decimals is similar to working with whole numbers.

Example:

Put 6.529, 6.531, and 6.526 in order from greatest to least.

Steps:

1. Align the numbers along the decimal point. 6.529
   6.531
   6.526

2. Work from left to right. In this problem, start by comparing the ones place.

3. If all the digits are the same, move to the next place.

4. In the hundredths place, 3 > 2 so 6.531 is the greatest number.

5. In the thousandths place, 9 > 6 so 6.529 is greater than 6.526.

6. .531, 6.529, and 6.526 are in order from greatest to least.

Directions: Select 5 meteors with decimal numbers that fall between the two numbers on the rockets. Order them from least to greatest, and write them on the planet.

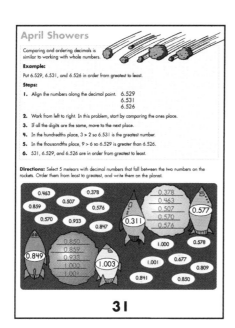

31

Compare the Decimals

Directions: Write >, <, or = in each ◯

1. 6.5 > 6.4   0.95 < 0.96   7.40 = 7.4

2. 0.86 > 0.859   9.02 < 9.20   8.51 > 8.5

3. 12.6 > 1.26   6.18 < 6.20   0.03 < 0.3

4. 1.863 > 1.862   4.32 > 4.23   5.2 > 5.1999

5. 3.046 < 3.406   7.419 > 6.42   45.3 > 45.28

6. 45.3 > 45.28   14.602 < 14.62   1.1406 < 1.146

7. 82.9 < 83.0   11.060 = 11.06   3.064 = 3.064

8. 0.523 < 0.530   12.0 > 11.91   1.351 < 13.51

Directions: Write the decimals from the least to the greatest on the ladders. Start at the bottom.

8.357, 8.35, 8.361, 8.36   12.310, 12.301, 12.013, 12.130

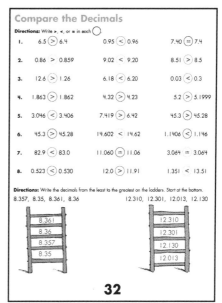

8.361
8.36
8.357
8.35

12.310
12.301
12.130
12.013

32

In the Sky

Directions: Complete each number to make the expression true.

1. 0.30___9 < 0.3019   0.___45 > 0.29   34.3___ < 35.37

2. 16.788 < 16.7___8   8.42___ > 8.427   ___067 < 1.0671

3. 3.416 > ___416   ___9___ < 0.08184   0.03243 < 0.03___2

4. 5.345 > 5.___4   *Answers will vary.*   178.___71 > 178.789

5. 3.99___ < 3.999   2.527 > 2.___48   17.098 > 1.___908

6. 2.0___3 > 1.999   17.6 > 1.___06   2___7.095 < 217.099

Directions: Write the decimals in order from least to greatest.

7. 16.39; 16.8; 16.7; 16.79
    16.39   16.7   16.79   16.8

8. 72.59; 56.56; 73.1; 56.6; 72.48
    56.56   56.6   72.48   72.59   73.1

9. 0.06; 0.6; 6.060; 0.006
    0.006   0.06   0.6   6.060

10. 109.041; 104.091; 401.001
    104.091   109.041   401.001

11. 5.5508; 5.5880; 5.58; 5.56
    5.5508   5.56   5.58   5.5880

33

May Flowers

Rounding decimals is the same as rounding whole numbers.

Example:

Round 4.386 to the nearest tenth.

Steps:

1. Underline the place to round and look at the digit one place to the right.   4.386

2. If this digit is less than 5, the digit you are rounding to stays the same. If the digit you are rounding to is greater than or equal to 5, add 1 to the place value.

4.386 is 4.4 rounded to the nearest tenth.

Directions: Round the numbers on each flower to the nearest ones, tenths, and hundredths. Write the rounded numbers on the petals.

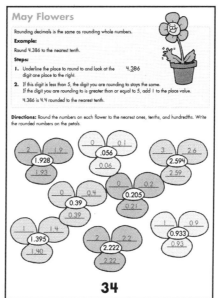

34

Order, Please!

Directions: Frank worked for his sister at the school snack shop. In one hour, he took orders for 20 items. He had to keep track of prices in his head, so he decided to round the prices. Help Frank round each price. Write the number on the price tag.

1. Round to the nearest dollar.

$1.00 — $1.44 hamburger $2.00 — $1.63 ham sandwich $2.00 — $2.37 jumbo french fries

2. Round to the nearest tenth.

$2.50 — $2.46 apple pie $0.30 — $0.34 peach $1.20 — $1.19 strawberries

3. Round to the nearest whole number.

$6.00 — $6.35 special meal deal $13.00 — $12.59 value meal $6.00 — $5.99 hot dog meal

4. Round to the nearest whole number.

$1.00 — $1.29 jumbo popcorn $3.00 — $2.54 giant cookie $1.00 — $0.62 brownie

35

Adding Decimals

Adding decimals is a lot like adding whole numbers. Be sure to align the decimal points.

CORRECT	INCORRECT
5.349	5.349
+ 34.322	+ 34.322
39.671	87.812

If the numbers being added do not have the same number of decimal places, write an equivalent decimal. Equivalent decimals are two decimals with the same value.

Examples: 0.29 = 0.290   1.4 = 1.400   3 = 3.000

Adding zeros to the right of the last decimal digit does not change the value of the number.

Example: 13.83 + 1.264 → 13.830
     + 1.264
     15.094

Directions: If all the decimals are equivalent, write a ✔ in the box. If not, write an **X**.

4.2   4.20   4.200 ✔   3.05   3.5   3.005 X

0.080   0.08   0.0800 ✔   9.000   9   9.0 ✔

0.77   0.7   0.777 X   1.6   1.06   1.60 X

Directions: Write an equivalent decimal for each number.

1.9 __1.90__   0.040 __0.04__   8 __8.00__   0.3 __0.30__

7.82 __7.820__   4.02 __4.020__   0.90 __0.900__   5 __5.0__

36

Subtracting Decimals

Steps:

1. Align the decimal points.

2. Write an equivalent number if necessary.

3. Subtract as with whole numbers.

15.865
− 3.272
12.593

Examples:

15.865 − 3.272 → 15.865
    − 3.272
    12.593

3.44 − 0.538 → 3.440
    − 0.538
    2.902

2 − 1.894 → 2.000
    − 1.894
    0.106

Directions: Subtract the lesser number from the greater one. Show your work in the space below.

1. 1.11   1.111 __0.001__   1.321   4.4 __3.079__

0.41   0.001 __0.409__   8.39   7 __1.39__

12.304   12.403 __0.099__   107.65   67.293 __40.357__

4   2.078 __1.922__   3.7   106.35 __102.65__

0.89   1.6 __0.71__   0.034   0.034 __0__

37

---

   75   *Master Math: Introductory Geometry*

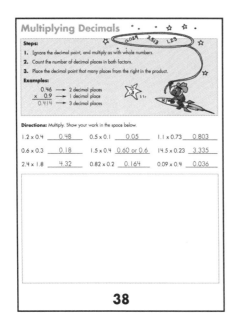

Multiplying Decimals

Steps:
1. Ignore the decimal point, and multiply as with whole numbers.
2. Count the number of decimal places in both factors.
3. Place the decimal point that many places from the right in the product.

Examples:

$$0.46 \rightarrow \text{2 decimal places}$$
$$\times\ 0.9 \rightarrow \text{1 decimal place}$$
$$0.414 \rightarrow \text{3 decimal places}$$

Directions: Multiply. Show your work in the space below.

1.2 × 0.4 __0.48__	0.5 × 0.1 __0.05__	1.1 × 0.73 __0.803__
0.6 × 0.3 __0.18__	1.5 × 0.4 __0.60 or 0.6__	14.5 × 0.23 __3.335__
2.4 × 1.8 __4.32__	0.82 × 0.2 __0.164__	0.09 × 0.4 __0.036__

38

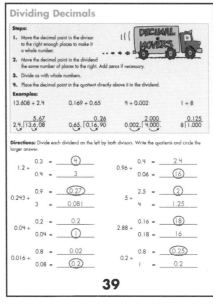

Dividing Decimals

Steps:
1. Move the decimal point in the divisor to the right enough places to make it a whole number.
2. Move the decimal point in the dividend the same number of places to the right. Add zeros if necessary.
3. Divide as with whole numbers.
4. Place the decimal point in the quotient directly above it in the dividend.

Examples:

13.608 ÷ 2.4   0.169 ÷ 0.65   4 ÷ 0.002   1 ÷ 8

$$2.4\overline{)13.6.08}\ \ \frac{5.67}{}\quad 0.65\overline{)0.16.90}\ \ \frac{0.26}{}\quad 0.002\overline{)4.000.}\ \ \frac{2.000}{}\quad 8\overline{)1.000}\ \ \frac{0.125}{}$$

Directions: Divide each dividend on the left by both divisors. Write the quotients and circle the larger answer.

1.2 ÷	0.3 = (4)	0.96 ÷	0.4 = 2.4
	0.4 = 3		0.06 = (16)
0.243 ÷	0.9 = (0.27)	5 ÷	2.5 = (2)
	3 = 0.081		4 = 1.25
0.04 ÷	0.2 = 0.2	2.88 ÷	0.16 = (18)
	0.04 = (1)		0.18 = 16
0.016 ÷	0.8 = 0.02	0.2 ÷	0.8 = (0.25)
	0.08 = (0.2)		1 = 0.2

39

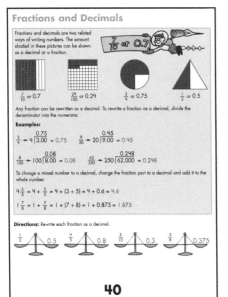

Fractions and Decimals

Fractions and decimals are two related ways of writing numbers. The amount shaded in these pictures can be shown as a decimal or a fraction.

$\frac{7}{10}$ or 0.7 $\frac{24}{100}$ or 0.24 $\frac{3}{4}$ or 0.75 $\frac{1}{2}$ or 0.5

Any fraction can be rewritten as a decimal. To rewrite a fraction as a decimal, divide the denominator into the numerator.

Examples:

$\frac{3}{4} \rightarrow 4\overline{)3.00}\ \frac{0.75}{} = 0.75$ $\frac{9}{20} \rightarrow 20\overline{)9.00}\ \frac{0.45}{} = 0.45$

$\frac{8}{100} \rightarrow 100\overline{)8.00}\ \frac{0.08}{} = 0.08$ $\frac{62}{250} \rightarrow 250\overline{)62.000}\ \frac{0.248}{} = 0.248$

To change a mixed number to a decimal, change the fraction part to a decimal and add it to the whole number.

$4\frac{3}{5} = 4 + \frac{3}{5} = 4 + (3 \div 5) = 4 + 0.6 = 4.6$

$1\frac{7}{8} = 1 + \frac{7}{8} = 1 + (7 \div 8) = 1 + 0.875 = 1.875$

Directions: Rewrite each fraction as a decimal.

$\frac{1}{2}$ 0.5 $\frac{4}{5}$ 0.8 $\frac{3}{10}$ 0.3 $\frac{3}{8}$ 0.375

40

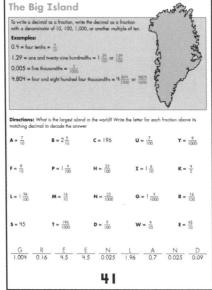

The Big Island

To write a decimal as a fraction, write the decimal as a fraction with a denominator of 10, 100, 1,000, or another multiple of ten.

Examples:

0.4 = four tenths = $\frac{4}{10}$

1.29 = one and twenty-nine hundredths = $1\frac{29}{100}$ or $\frac{129}{100}$

0.005 = five thousandths = $\frac{5}{1000}$

4.804 = four and eight hundred four thousandths = $4\frac{804}{1000}$ or $\frac{4804}{1000}$

Directions: What is the largest island in the world? Write the letter for each fraction above its matching decimal to decode the answer.

A = $\frac{7}{10}$	**B** = $2\frac{5}{10}$	**C** = 196	**U** = $\frac{7}{100}$	**Y** = $\frac{9}{1000}$
F = $\frac{9}{10}$	**P** = $1\frac{4}{100}$	**H** = $\frac{25}{100}$	**I** = $1\frac{6}{10}$	**K** = $\frac{4}{5}$
L = $1\frac{96}{100}$	**M** = $\frac{16}{10}$	**N** = $\frac{25}{1000}$	**G** = $1\frac{4}{100}$	**R** = $\frac{16}{100}$
S = 45	**T** = $\frac{196}{1000}$	**D** = $\frac{9}{10}$	**W** = $\frac{4}{10}$	**E** = $\frac{45}{10}$

G	R	E	E	N	L	A	N	D
1.004	0.16	4.5	4.5	0.025	1.96	0.7	0.025	0.09

41

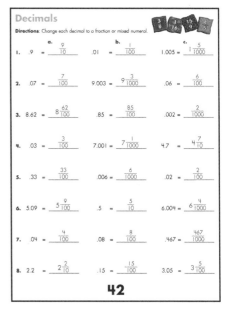

Decimals

Directions: Change each decimal to a fraction or mixed numeral.

	a.	b.	c.
1. .9 = $\frac{9}{10}$	.01 = $\frac{1}{100}$	1.005 = $1\frac{5}{1000}$
2. .07 = $\frac{7}{100}$	9.003 = $9\frac{3}{1000}$	.06 = $\frac{6}{100}$
3. 8.62 = $8\frac{62}{100}$	.85 = $\frac{85}{100}$	.002 = $\frac{2}{1000}$
4. .03 = $\frac{3}{100}$	7.001 = $7\frac{1}{1000}$	4.7 = $4\frac{7}{10}$
5. .33 = $\frac{33}{100}$	.006 = $\frac{6}{1000}$	.02 = $\frac{2}{100}$
6. 5.09 = $5\frac{9}{100}$	.5 = $\frac{5}{10}$	6.004 = $6\frac{4}{1000}$
7. .04 = $\frac{4}{100}$	.08 = $\frac{8}{100}$	.467 = $\frac{467}{1000}$
8. 2.2 = $2\frac{2}{10}$	.15 = $\frac{15}{100}$	3.05 = $3\frac{5}{100}$

42

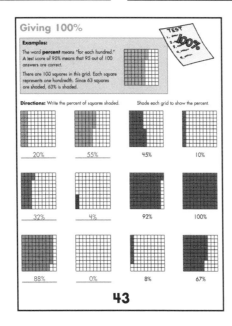

Giving 100%

Examples:

The word **percent** means "for each hundred." A test score of 95% means that 95 out of 100 answers are correct.

There are 100 squares in this grid. Each square represents one hundredth. Since 63 squares are shaded, 63% is shaded.

Directions: Write the percent of squares shaded.   Shade each grid to show the percent.

20%	55%	45%	10%
32%	4%	92%	100%
88%	0%	8%	67%

43

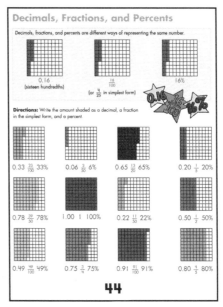

Decimals, Fractions, and Percents

Decimals, fractions, and percents are different ways of representing the same number.

0.16 $\frac{16}{100}$ 16%
(sixteen hundredths)   (or $\frac{4}{25}$ in simplest form)

Directions: Write the amount shaded as a decimal, a fraction in the simplest form, and a percent.

0.33 $\frac{33}{100}$ 33%	0.06 $\frac{3}{50}$ 6%	0.65 $\frac{13}{20}$ 65%	0.20 $\frac{1}{5}$ 20%
0.78 $\frac{39}{50}$ 78%	1.00 1 100%	0.22 $\frac{11}{50}$ 22%	0.50 $\frac{1}{2}$ 50%
0.49 $\frac{49}{100}$ 49%	0.75 $\frac{3}{4}$ 75%	0.91 $\frac{91}{100}$ 91%	0.80 $\frac{4}{5}$ 80%

44

Percents and Decimals

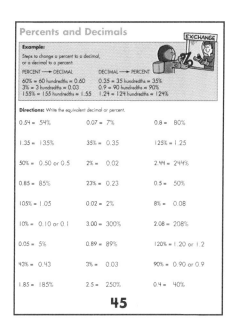

Example:
Steps to change a percent to a decimal, or a decimal to a percent.

PERCENT → DECIMAL	DECIMAL → PERCENT
60% = 60 hundredths = 0.60	0.35 = 35 hundredths = 35%
3% = 3 hundredths = 0.03	0.9 = 90 hundredths = 90%
155% = 155 hundredths = 1.55	1.24 = 124 hundredths = 124%

Directions: Write the equivalent decimal or percent.

0.54 = 54%	0.07 = 7%	0.8 = 80%
1.35 = 135%	35% = 0.35	125% = 1.25
50% = 0.50 or 0.5	2% = 0.02	2.44 = 244%
0.85 = 85%	23% = 0.23	0.5 = 50%
105% = 1.05	0.02 = 2%	8% = 0.08
10% = 0.10 or 0.1	3.00 = 300%	2.08 = 208%
0.05 = 5%	0.89 = 89%	120% = 1.20 or 1.2
43% = 0.43	3% = 0.03	90% = 0.90 or 0.9
1.85 = 185%	2.5 = 250%	0.4 = 40%

45

Presto Change-o!

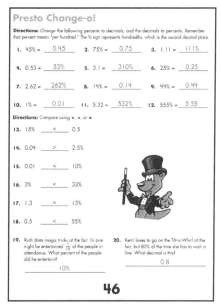

Directions: Change the following percents to decimals, and the decimals to percents. Remember that percent means "per hundred." The % sign represents hundredths, which is the second decimal place.

1. 45% = 0.45
2. 75% = 0.75
3. 1.11 = 111%
4. 0.53 = 53%
5. 3.1 = 310%
6. 25% = 0.25
7. 2.62 = 262%
8. 14% = 0.14
9. 44% = 0.44
10. 1% = 0.01
11. 5.32 = 532%
12. 555% = 5.55

Directions: Compare using >, <, or =.

13. 15% < 0.5
14. 0.04 > 2.5%
15. 0.01 < 10%
16. 3% < 33%
17. 1.3 > 13%
18. 0.5 < 55%

19. Rudi does magic tricks at the fair. In one night he entertained $\frac{1}{10}$ of the people in attendance. What percent of the people did he entertain?
10%

20. Kerri loves to go on the Tilt-a-Whirl at the fair, but 80% of the time she has to wait in line. What decimal is this?
0.8

46

Lots of Nests

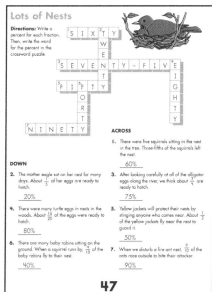

Directions: Write a percent for each fraction. Then, write the word for the percent in the crossword puzzle.

```
S I X T Y
      W
      E
S E V E N T Y - F I V E
      T        I
F I F T Y     G
      O        H
      R        T
      T        Y
N I N E T Y
```

DOWN

2. The mother eagle sat on her nest for many days. About $\frac{1}{5}$ of her eggs are ready to hatch.
20%

4. There were many turtle eggs in nests in the woods. About $\frac{16}{20}$ of the eggs are ready to hatch.
80%

6. There are many baby robins sitting on the ground. When a squirrel runs by, $\frac{4}{10}$ of the baby robins fly to their nest.
40%

ACROSS

1. There were five squirrels sitting in the nest in the tree. Three-fifths of the squirrels left the nest.
60%

3. After looking carefully at all of the alligator eggs along the river, we think about $\frac{3}{4}$ are ready to hatch.
75%

5. Yellow jackets will protect their nests by stinging anyone who comes near. About $\frac{1}{2}$ of the yellow jackets fly near the nest to guard it.
50%

7. When we disturb a fire ant nest, $\frac{9}{10}$ of the ants race outside to bite their attacker.
90%

47

Simplified Percents

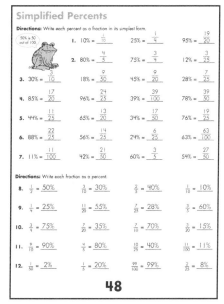

Directions: Write each percent as a fraction in its simplest form.

50% = 50 out of 100

1. 10% = $\frac{1}{10}$ 25% = $\frac{1}{4}$ 95% = $\frac{19}{20}$
2. 80% = $\frac{4}{5}$ 75% = $\frac{3}{4}$ 12% = $\frac{3}{25}$
3. 30% = $\frac{3}{10}$ 18% = $\frac{9}{50}$ 45% = $\frac{9}{20}$ 28% = $\frac{7}{25}$
4. 85% = $\frac{17}{20}$ 96% = $\frac{24}{25}$ 39% = $\frac{39}{100}$ 78% = $\frac{39}{50}$
5. 44% = $\frac{11}{25}$ 65% = $\frac{13}{20}$ 34% = $\frac{17}{50}$ 76% = $\frac{19}{25}$
6. 88% = $\frac{22}{25}$ 56% = $\frac{14}{25}$ 24% = $\frac{6}{25}$ 63% = $\frac{63}{100}$
7. 11% = $\frac{11}{100}$ 42% = $\frac{21}{50}$ 60% = $\frac{3}{5}$ 54% = $\frac{27}{50}$

Directions: Write each fraction as a percent.

8. $\frac{1}{2}$ = 50% $\frac{3}{10}$ = 30% $\frac{2}{5}$ = 40% $\frac{1}{10}$ = 10%
9. $\frac{1}{4}$ = 25% $\frac{11}{20}$ = 55% $\frac{7}{25}$ = 28% $\frac{3}{5}$ = 60%
10. $\frac{3}{4}$ = 75% $\frac{7}{20}$ = 35% $\frac{7}{10}$ = 70% $\frac{3}{20}$ = 15%
11. $\frac{9}{10}$ = 90% $\frac{4}{5}$ = 80% $\frac{10}{25}$ = 40% $\frac{11}{100}$ = 11%
12. $\frac{1}{50}$ = 2% $\frac{1}{5}$ = 20% $\frac{99}{100}$ = 99% $\frac{2}{25}$ = 8%

48

Let's Go Exploring

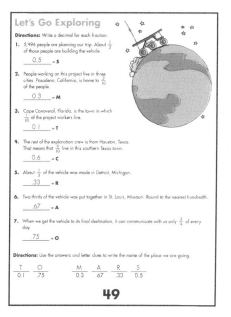

Directions: Write a decimal for each fraction.

1. 5,496 people are planning our trip. About $\frac{1}{2}$ of those people are building the vehicle.
0.5 = S

2. People working on this project live in three cities. Pasadena, California, is home to $\frac{3}{10}$ of the people.
0.3 = M

3. Cape Canaveral, Florida, is the town in which $\frac{1}{10}$ of the project workers live.
0.1 = T

4. The rest of the exploration crew is from Houston, Texas. That means that $\frac{6}{10}$ live in this southern Texas town.
0.6 = C

5. About $\frac{1}{3}$ of the vehicle was made in Detroit, Michigan.
.33 = R

6. Two-thirds of the vehicle was put together in St. Louis, Missouri. Round to the nearest hundredth.
.67 = A

7. When we get the vehicle to its final destination, it can communicate with us only $\frac{3}{4}$ of every day.
.75 = O

Directions: Use the answers and letter clues to write the name of the place we are going.

T	O		M	A	R	S
0.1	.75		0.3	.67	.33	0.5

49

Percents and Fractions

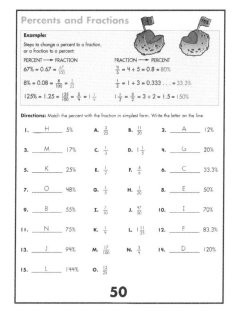

Example:
Steps to change a percent to a fraction, or a fraction to a percent.

PERCENT → FRACTION	FRACTION → PERCENT
67% = 0.67 = $\frac{67}{100}$	$\frac{4}{5}$ = 4 ÷ 5 = 0.8 = 80%
8% = 0.08 = $\frac{8}{100}$ = $\frac{2}{25}$	$\frac{1}{3}$ = 1 ÷ 3 = 0.333 . . . = 33.3%
125% = 1.25 = $\frac{125}{100}$ = $\frac{5}{4}$ = 1$\frac{1}{4}$	1$\frac{1}{2}$ = $\frac{3}{2}$ = 3 ÷ 2 = 1.5 = 150%

Directions: Match the percent with the fraction in simplest form. Write the letter on the line.

1. H 5%   A. $\frac{3}{25}$ B. $\frac{11}{20}$ 2. A 12%
3. M 17%   C. $\frac{1}{3}$ D. 1$\frac{1}{5}$ 4. G 20%
5. K 25%   E. $\frac{1}{2}$ F. $\frac{5}{6}$ 6. C 33.3%
7. O 48%   G. $\frac{1}{5}$ H. $\frac{1}{20}$ 8. E 50%
9. B 55%   I. $\frac{7}{10}$ J. $\frac{47}{50}$ 10. I 70%
11. N 75%   K. $\frac{1}{4}$ L. 1$\frac{11}{25}$ 12. F 83.3%
13. J 94%   M. $\frac{17}{100}$ N. $\frac{3}{4}$ 14. D 120%
15. L 144%   O. $\frac{12}{25}$

50

Percent of a Number

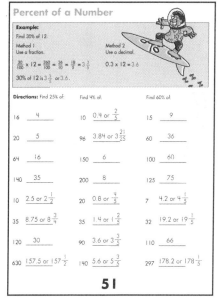

Example:
Find 30% of 12.

Method 1	Method 2
Use a fraction.	Use a decimal.
$\frac{30}{100}$ × 12 = $\frac{360}{100}$ = $\frac{36}{10}$ = $\frac{18}{5}$ = 3$\frac{3}{5}$	0.3 × 12 = 3.6

30% of 12 is 3$\frac{3}{5}$ or 3.6.

Directions: Find 25% of: Find 4% of: Find 60% of:

16	4	10	0.4 or $\frac{2}{5}$	15	9
20	5	96	3.84 or 3$\frac{21}{25}$	60	36
64	16	150	6	100	60
140	35	200	8	125	75
10	2.5 or 2$\frac{1}{2}$	20	0.8 or $\frac{4}{5}$	7	4.2 or 4$\frac{1}{5}$
35	8.75 or 8$\frac{3}{4}$	35	1.4 or 1$\frac{2}{5}$	32	19.2 or 19$\frac{1}{5}$
120	30	90	3.6 or 3$\frac{3}{5}$	110	66
630	157.5 or 157$\frac{1}{2}$	140	5.6 or 5$\frac{3}{5}$	297	178.2 or 178$\frac{1}{5}$

51

Abstract Art

Directions: The grid below contains 100 squares. Each square represents 0.01 or $\frac{1}{100}$ or 1% of all the squares. Use the table below to complete and color in the grid to achieve your own unique design.

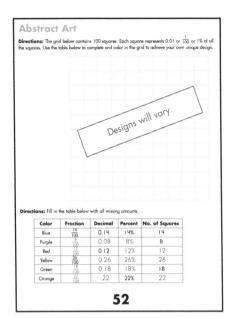

Designs will vary.

Directions: Fill in the table below with all missing amounts.

Color	Fraction	Decimal	Percent	No. of Squares
Blue	$\frac{14}{100}$	0.14	14%	14
Purple	$\frac{8}{100}$	0.08	8%	8
Red	$\frac{12}{100}$	0.12	12%	12
Yellow	$\frac{26}{100}$	0.26	26%	26
Green	$\frac{18}{100}$	0.18	18%	18
Orange	$\frac{22}{100}$	.22	22%	22

52

Wacky Expressions

Directions: Turn these circles into expressive faces by drawing the correct features on the circles. Match the fraction under each circle with the correct decimal, reduced fraction, and percent below.

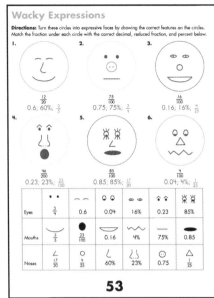

1. $\frac{12}{20}$ 0.6; 60%; $\frac{3}{5}$
2. $\frac{75}{100}$ 0.75; 75%; $\frac{3}{4}$
3. $\frac{16}{100}$ 0.16; 16%; $\frac{4}{25}$
4. $\frac{46}{200}$ 0.23; 23%; $\frac{23}{100}$
5. $\frac{85}{100}$ 0.85; 85%; $\frac{17}{20}$
6. $\frac{4}{100}$ 0.04; 4%; $\frac{1}{25}$

Eyes	$\frac{3}{4}$	0.6	0.04	16%	0.23	85%
Mouths	$\frac{3}{5}$		$\frac{23}{100}$	0.16	4%	75%	0.85
Noses	$\frac{17}{20}$	$\frac{4}{25}$	60%	23%	0.75	$\frac{1}{23}$

53

Flocking Together

Directions: In Australia, huge trees are filled with birds at sunset. Although it can be hard to see these birds at first, you can always hear them! Write a decimal and a percent for each fraction.

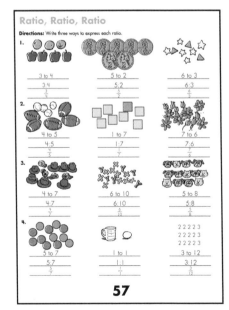

1. Of the parrots in the tree, $\frac{8}{12}$ were green. Round to the nearest hundredth.

   .67; 67%

2. Four-twelfths of the parrots in the tree were blue.

   .33; 33%

3. Five flocks of cockatoos landed in the tree just as the sun set. Four-fifths of these birds were white with yellow crests on their heads.

   0.8; 80%

4. Three-fifths of the pink cockatoos were less than two years old.

   0.6; 60%

5. Of the black cockatoos in the tree, $\frac{3}{4}$ sat at the top of the tree.

   .75; 75%

6. Five twenty-fifths of the black cockatoos watch the skies for danger.

   0.2; 20%

7. When the sun rises, $\frac{2}{5}$ of the birds in the tree fly away looking for food.

   0.4; 40%

54

Many Names—One Amount

Directions: Complete the table.

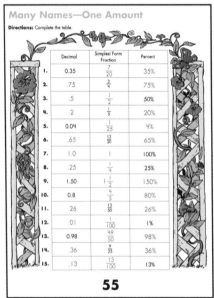

	Decimal	Simplest Form Fraction	Percent
1.	0.35	$\frac{7}{20}$	35%
2.	.75	$\frac{3}{4}$	75%
3.	.5	$\frac{1}{2}$	50%
4.	.2	$\frac{1}{5}$	20%
5.	0.04	$\frac{1}{25}$	4%
6.	.65	$\frac{13}{20}$	65%
7.	1.0	1	100%
8.	.25	$\frac{1}{4}$	25%
9.	1.50	$1\frac{1}{2}$	150%
10.	0.8	$\frac{4}{5}$	80%
11.	.26	$\frac{13}{50}$	26%
12.	.01	$\frac{1}{100}$	1%
13.	0.98	$\frac{49}{50}$	98%
14.	.36	$\frac{9}{25}$	36%
15.	.13	$\frac{13}{100}$	13%

55

Ratios

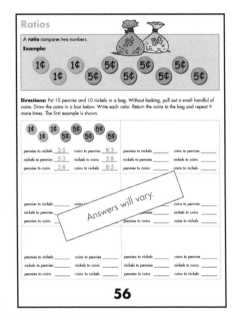

A **ratio** compares two numbers.
Example:

Directions: Put 10 pennies and 10 nickels in a bag. Without looking, pull out a small handful of coins. Draw the coins in a box below. Write each ratio. Return the coins to the bag and repeat 4 more times. The first example is shown.

pennies to nickels 3:5   coins to pennies 8:3   pennies to nickels ____   coins to pennies ____
nickels to pennies 5:3   nickels to coins 5:8   nickels to pennies ____   nickels to coins ____
pennies to coins 3:8   nickels to coins 8:5   pennies to coins ____   coins to nickels ____

Answers will vary.

pennies to nickels ____   coins to pennies ____   pennies to nickels ____   coins to pennies ____
nickels to pennies ____   nickels to coins ____   nickels to pennies ____   nickels to coins ____
pennies to coins ____   coins to nickels ____   pennies to coins ____   coins to nickels ____

pennies to nickels ____   coins to pennies ____   pennies to nickels ____   coins to pennies ____
nickels to pennies ____   nickels to coins ____   nickels to pennies ____   nickels to coins ____
pennies to coins ____   coins to nickels ____   pennies to coins ____   coins to nickels ____

56

Ratio, Ratio, Ratio

Directions: Write three ways to express each ratio.

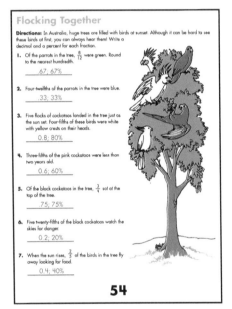

1.
   3 to 4 | 5 to 2 | 6 to 3
   3:4 | 5:2 | 6:3
   $\frac{3}{4}$ | $\frac{5}{2}$ | $\frac{6}{3}$

2.
   4 to 5 | 1 to 7 | 7 to 6
   4:5 | 1:7 | 7:6
   $\frac{4}{5}$ | $\frac{1}{7}$ | $\frac{7}{6}$

3.
   4 to 7 | 6 to 10 | 5 to 8
   4:7 | 6:10 | 5:8
   $\frac{4}{7}$ | $\frac{6}{10}$ | $\frac{5}{8}$

4.
   5 to 7 | 1 to 1 | 3 to 12
   5:7 | 1:1 | 3:12
   $\frac{5}{7}$ | $\frac{1}{1}$ | $\frac{3}{12}$

57

Working With Ratios

A ratio is a comparison of two numbers. There are several ways to express a ratio.

12 out of 20   12 to 20   12:20 $\frac{12}{20} = \frac{3}{5}$

Directions: Fill in the blank spaces on the table below.

	Verbal description	a to b	a:b	$\frac{a}{b}$ (simplified)
1.	10 out of 15	10 to 15	10:15	$\frac{2}{3}$
2.	6 out of 20	6 to 20	6:20	$\frac{3}{10}$
3.	9 out of 10	9 to 10	9:10	$\frac{9}{10}$
4.	5 out of 50	5 to 50	5:50	$\frac{1}{10}$
5.	16 out of 48	16 to 48	16:48	$\frac{1}{3}$
6.	3 out of 8	3 to 8	3:8	$\frac{3}{8}$
7.	13 out of 52	13 to 52	13:52	$\frac{1}{4}$
8.	18 out of 90	18 to 90	18:90	$\frac{1}{5}$
9.	15 out of 45	15 to 45	15:45	$\frac{1}{3}$
10.	3 out of 7	3 to 7	3:7	$\frac{3}{7}$
11.	4 out of 11	4 to 11	4:11	$\frac{4}{11}$
12.	105 out of 150	105 to 150	105:150	$\frac{7}{10}$
13.	8 out of 12	8 to 12	8:12	$\frac{2}{3}$

58

Proportions

Another way of writing a ratio is as a fraction. 3:7 is the same as $\frac{3}{7}$. Remember what you have learned about cross multiplication. $\frac{3}{7} \times \frac{4}{8}$

Because the products of cross multiplication are the same, the fractions are equivalent. When two ratios or fractions are equivalent, they form a **proportion**.

Example:

Steps to find an unknown term of a proportion:

Lisa uses 2 pots to plant 8 seeds.
How many pots will she need to plant 24 seeds?

1. Write a proportion. $\frac{2 \text{ pots}}{8 \text{ seeds}} = \frac{n \text{ pots}}{24 \text{ seeds}}$

2. Cross multiply. $\frac{2}{8} \times \frac{n}{24}$

$8 \times n = 48$
$n = 6$ (Divide both sides of the proportion by 8.)
Lisa needs 6 pots to plant 24 seeds.

Directions: If the ratios form a proportion, write **yes** on the line. If not, write **no**.

$\frac{4}{5} = \frac{24}{30}$ __yes__ $\frac{1}{2} = \frac{36}{72}$ __yes__ $\frac{3}{7} = \frac{20}{35}$ __no__ $\frac{1}{23} = \frac{8}{184}$ __yes__

$\frac{6}{13} = \frac{75}{156}$ __no__ $\frac{9}{5} = \frac{171}{95}$ __yes__ $\frac{4}{21} = \frac{40}{210}$ __yes__ $\frac{11}{12} = \frac{154}{168}$ __yes__

Directions: Find the unknown term in each of these proportions.

$\frac{4}{5} = \frac{n}{15}$ __12__ $\frac{n}{104} = \frac{5}{13}$ __40__ $\frac{5}{6} = \frac{45}{n}$ __54__

59

Ratio and Proportion

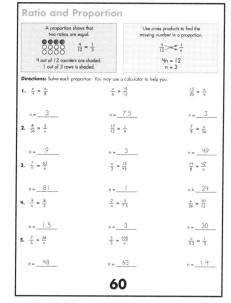

A proportion shows that two ratios are equal.

$\frac{4}{12} = \frac{1}{3}$

4 out of 12 counters are shaded.
1 out of 3 rows is shaded.

Use cross products to find the missing number in a proportion.

$\frac{4}{12} \times \frac{n}{3}$

$4n = 12$
$n = 3$

Directions: Solve each proportion. You may use a calculator to help you.

1. $\frac{n}{4} = \frac{6}{8}$ $\frac{6}{n} = \frac{15}{12}$ $\frac{15}{20} = \frac{n}{4}$

    n = __3__   n = __7.5__   n = __3__

2. $\frac{8}{36} = \frac{2}{n}$ $\frac{15}{12} = \frac{n}{4}$ $\frac{7}{8} = \frac{n}{56}$

    n = __9__   n = __5__   n = __49__

3. $\frac{7}{9} = \frac{63}{n}$ $\frac{n}{3} = \frac{15}{45}$ $\frac{14}{8} = \frac{42}{n}$

    n = __81__   n = __1__   n = __24__

4. $\frac{4}{n} = \frac{8}{3}$ $\frac{2}{n} = \frac{8}{75}$ $\frac{n}{39} = \frac{10}{13}$

    n = __1.5__   n = __3__   n = __30__

5. $\frac{7}{6} = \frac{56}{n}$ $\frac{5}{3} = \frac{105}{n}$ $\frac{n}{42} = \frac{1}{3}$

    n = __48__   n = __63__   n = __1.4__

60

What Are the Chances?

Probability is the chance that something will happen.

Example:

This spinner has 8 equal-sized spaces. What is the probability, or chance, that a person would spin:

Blue? $\frac{4}{8}$ or 4:8, because 4 of 8 sections are blue.

Red? $\frac{1}{8}$ or 1:8, because 1 of 8 sections is red.

Yellow? $\frac{2}{8}$ or 2:8, because 2 of 8 sections are yellow.

Green? $\frac{1}{8}$ or 1:8, because 1 of 8 sections is green.

Directions: Use the spinner to the right to answer the questions.

1. What is the probability of spinning blue? $\frac{2}{8}$

2. What is the probability of spinning yellow? $\frac{2}{8}$

3. What is the probability of spinning green? $\frac{4}{8}$

4. What is the probability of spinning yellow or red? $\frac{4}{8}$

Directions: Use the spinner to the right to answer the questions.

1. What is the probability of spinning purple? $\frac{2}{6}$

2. What is the probability of spinning orange? $\frac{2}{6}$

3. What is the probability of spinning yellow? $\frac{2}{6}$

4. What is the probability of spinning yellow, orange, or purple? $\frac{6}{6}$

Directions: Use the spinner to the right to answer the questions.

1. What is the probability of spinning a 4? $\frac{3}{6}$

2. What is the probability of spinning a 1? $\frac{1}{6}$

3. What is the probability of spinning a 3? $\frac{1}{6}$

4. What is the probability of spinning 3, 4, or 6? $\frac{4}{6}$

61

Photo Safari

Directions: The students at Carver School are going to take pictures of wildlife. Help the students find the probability. Write each fraction. Reduce the fraction to its lowest terms, if necessary.

1. The first trip was to the woods. Stella startled a group of 3 raccoons, 2 skunks, 4 opossums, and 1 weasel. She took a picture quickly without really looking.

   What is the probability Stella photographed a weasel? $\frac{1}{10}$

   What is the probability she photographed a skunk? $\frac{2}{10}$

   What is the probability she photographed an opossum? $\frac{4}{10}$

   What is the probability she photographed a raccoon? $\frac{3}{10}$

2. Livingston doesn't know it, but he's surrounded by 6 flying squirrels, 4 bats, 7 owls, and 3 night herons.

   If he looks up, what is the probability he will see an owl? $\frac{7}{20}$

   What is the probability he will see a flying squirrel? $\frac{6}{20}$

   What is the probability he will see a bat? $\frac{4}{20}$

   What is the probability he will see a night heron? $\frac{3}{20}$

3. Jasmin likes animals that crawl. In the soil where she is waiting, there are 3 night crawlers, 2 centipedes, 1 ant lion, and 4 beetles.

   What is the probability she will see an ant lion? $\frac{1}{10}$

   What is the probability she will see a beetle? $\frac{4}{10}$

   What is the probability she will see a centipede? $\frac{2}{10}$

   What is the probability she will see a night crawler? $\frac{3}{10}$

4. The next trip the students took was to the desert. More animals roam the desert at night, when it is cooler than during the daytime. Lamar rests on a rock. Nearby are 2 sidewinders, 5 scorpions, 4 kangaroo rats, and 3 owls.

   What is the probability he will see a scorpion? $\frac{5}{14}$

   What is the probability he will see a sidewinder? $\frac{2}{14}$

   What is the probability he will see an owl? $\frac{3}{14}$

   What is the probability he will see a kangaroo rat? $\frac{4}{14}$

62

Likely and Unlikely

The probability of an event happening can be written as a fraction from 0 and 1.

Example:

Certain if the probability is 1.   The probability of spinning red, blue, or green is $\frac{6}{6}$ or 1.

More likely if its probability is greater than another.   It is more likely to spin green ($\frac{3}{6}$) than red ($\frac{2}{6}$).

Less likely if its probability is less than another.   It is less likely to spin blue ($\frac{1}{6}$) than red ($\frac{2}{6}$).

Equally likely if the probabilities are the same.   It is equally likely to spin red or blue ($\frac{2}{6}$) or green ($\frac{2}{6}$).

Impossible if the probability is 0.   It is impossible to spin white ($\frac{0}{6} = 0$).

Directions: Look at the spinner. Write the probability for each event below. Write **certain** or **impossible**, where appropriate.

spinning a 6 $\frac{0}{10}$; impossible   spinning a 4 $\frac{3}{10}$

spinning a 2 $\frac{1}{10}$ spinning a 4 or 5 $\frac{5}{10}$

spinning an even number $\frac{4}{10}$ spinning a prime number $\frac{6}{10}$

spinning a number < 10 $\frac{10}{10}$; certain   spinning a zero $\frac{0}{10}$; impossible

Directions: Look at the spinner to find which is **more likely**, **less likely**, or **equally likely**.

Spinning a 4 is __more likely__ than spinning a 5.

Spinning a 4 is __equally likely__ than spinning a 1.

Spinning an even number is __less likely__ than spinning an odd number.

63

Predicting Outcomes

To find the probability of an outcome, we must find the relative frequency of that outcome. This can be expressed as a ratio:

$$\frac{\text{frequency of outcome}}{\text{total frequency of all outcomes}}$$

We can also use this equation to predict future outcomes. Simply make an equality with **n** (the frequency) as an unknown number.

For example, if $\frac{12}{50}$ is the probability of having a rainy day out of 50 days, then $\frac{n}{100}$ might be the prediction of having **n** amount of rainy days out of 100 days.

$$\frac{4}{5} = \frac{24}{30}$$
$$n = 24$$

Directions: Solve the probability problems below.

1. If the probability of having rain is $\frac{8}{50}$, meaning that rain had fallen 8 out of the last 50 days, how many days would you expect it to rain out of the next 100?

   __n = 16__

2. Explain why using probability may or may not be a good way to predict the weather.

   __Answers will vary.__

3. If 32 out of 36 students pick red as their favorite color, what could you assume about the results of a sampling of 108 students?

   __96 will pick red.__

64

Playing Games

Directions: Solve the probability problems below.

1. A jar contains 4 blue marbles, 8 red marbles, 2 yellow marbles, and 12 orange marbles. Find the probability of:

   a. P (red or blue marble) $\frac{6}{13}$

   b. P (orange marble) $\frac{6}{13}$

   c. P (yellow or orange marble) $\frac{7}{13}$

   d. P (a marble) __1__

   e. P (a green marble) __0__

2. Marty and Chandra have played jacks during recess 18 out of the last 30 days. What is the probability that they will play jacks today? $\frac{3}{5}$

3. During indoor recess, Leah, Shalti, and Benny were allowed to play with either the pogo stick, the yo-yo, or the jump rope. In how many different ways can the students be matched to the toys? List them. Leah—pogo; Leah—yo-yo; Leah—jump rope; Shalti—pogo; Shalti—yo-yo; Shalti—jump rope; Benny—pogo; Benny—yo-yo; Benny—jump rope

4. Fifty students were surveyed. Forty preferred soccer to four-square. Predict how many students out of 200 would prefer soccer.

   __160__

5. For being star of the week, Justin may choose to play either jacks, go-fish, or solitaire, and he may choose a snack of popcorn or pretzels. What is the probability he will choose jacks and popcorn? $\frac{1}{6}$

65

Master Math: Introductory Geometry

Movie Time

Directions: Use the data in the table to make a circle graph.

Movie Viewing Preferences	
Comedy	$\frac{5}{12}$
Drama	$\frac{1}{12}$
Suspense	$\frac{2}{12}$
Science fiction	$\frac{4}{12}$

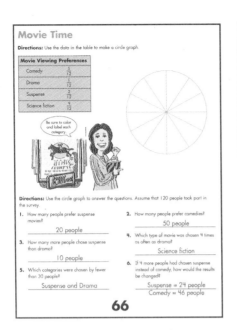

Be sure to color and label each category.

Directions: Use the circle graph to answer the questions. Assume that 120 people took part in the survey.

1. How many people prefer suspense movies?
   20 people

2. How many people prefer comedies?
   50 people

3. How many more people chose suspense than drama?
   10 people

4. Which type of movie was chosen 4 times as often as drama?
   Science fiction

5. Which categories were chosen by fewer than 30 people?
   Suspense and Drama

6. If 4 more people had chosen suspense instead of comedy, how would the results be changed?
   Suspense = 24 people
   Comedy = 46 people

66

Flying Forks

Directions: Look at a plastic fork. What do you think will happen if you drop the fork—will it land faceup, facedown, or on its side? What is the probability of each position?

PREDICT:

Imagine dropping the fork 50 different times. Predict how many times the fork will land:

Faceup: _example: 16 times_

Facedown: _example: 17 times_

On its side: _example: 17 times_

EXPERIMENT:

Drop the fork 50 times. Record how many times it lands in each position.

Faceup: _____

Facedown: _____

On its side: _____

ORGANIZE THE DATA:

Graph the results.

Answers will vary.

50
45
40
35
30
25
20
15
10
5
0
  Up   Down   Side

67

Scores and Statistics

Directions: Rewrite the data in order from least to greatest. Then, find the range, mean, median, and mode. Round to the nearest ten.

1. 79, 90, 85, 66, 77, 77, 91
   66 77 77 79 85 90 91
   Range: 25   Mean: 81
   Median: 79   Mode: 77

2. 86, 96, 59, 74, 59, 82, 70
   59 59 70 74 82 86 96
   Range: 37   Mean: 75
   Median: 74   Mode: 59

3. 83, 90, 54, 77, 54, 86, 72
   54 54 72 77 83 86 90
   Range: 36   Mean: 74
   Median: 77   Mode: 54

4. 72, 65, 36, 56, 87, 97, 65, 58
   36 56 58 65 65 72 87 97
   Range: 61   Mean: 67
   Median: 65   Mode: 65

5. 82, 57, 46, 67, 89, 97, 65, 55
   46 55 57 67 67 82 89 97
   Range: 51   Mean: 70
   Median: 67   Mode: 67

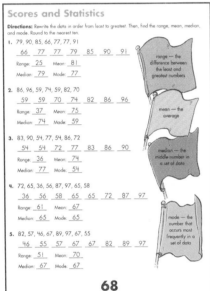

range — the difference between the least and greatest numbers

mean — the average

median — the middle number in a set of data

mode — the number that occurs most frequently in a set of data

68

Graphing Test Results

Directions: Use the data in the table to make a bar graph.

Sam's Test Score Averages	
English	95
Math	90
Social Studies	60
Science	80
Spanish	75
Health	70

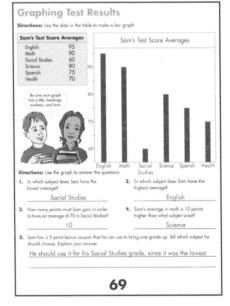

Be sure your graph has a title, headings, numbers, and bars.

Sam's Test Score Averages

90
80
70
60
English Math Social Studies Science Spanish Health

Directions: Use the graph to answer the questions.

1. In which subject does Sam have the lowest average?
   Social Studies

2. In which subject does Sam have the highest average?
   English

3. How many points must Sam gain in order to have an average of 70 in Social Studies?
   10

4. Sam's average in math is 10 points higher than what subject area?
   Science

5. Sam has a 5-point bonus coupon that he can use to bring one grade up. Tell which subject he should choose. Explain your answer.
   He should use it for his Social Studies grade, since it was the lowest.

69

What's the Vote?

Directions: Alyson's class is interested in growing a flower garden for the whole school to enjoy. To collect data on flower preferences, they surveyed the students in the school. Out of an enrollment of 435, the following resulted.

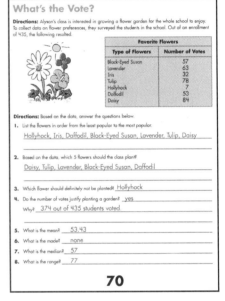

Favorite Flowers	
Type of Flowers	**Number of Votes**
Black-Eyed Susan	57
Lavender	63
Iris	32
Tulip	78
Hollyhock	7
Daffodil	53
Daisy	84

Directions: Based on the data, answer the questions below.

1. List the flowers in order from the least popular to the most popular.
   Hollyhock, Iris, Daffodil, Black-Eyed Susan, Lavender, Tulip, Daisy

2. Based on the data, which 5 flowers should the class plant?
   Daisy, Tulip, Lavender, Black-Eyed Susan, Daffodil

3. Which flower should definitely not be planted? **Hollyhock**

4. Do the number of votes justify planting a garden? **yes**
   Why? **374 out of 435 students voted.**

5. What is the mean? **53.43**
6. What is the mode? **none**
7. What is the median? **57**
8. What is the range? **77**

70